The Life and Crimes of Jared Flagg
Adventures of a Gilded Age Huckster, Swindler & Pimp

Eric B. Easton

The Life and Crimes of Jared Flagg

Adventures of a Gilded Age Huckster, Swindler & Pimp

Eric B. Easton

Academica Press
Washington~London

Library of Congress Cataloging-in-Publication Data

Names: Easton, Eric B. (author)
Title: The life and crimes of jared flagg : adventures of a gilded age huckster, swindler & pimp | Eric B. Easton
Description: Washington : Academica Press, 2021. | Includes references.
Identifiers: LCCN 2021936491 | ISBN 9781680538960 (hardcover) | 9781680538977 (paperback) | 9781680538984 (e-book)

Dedication

This book is dedicated to my mother and father,

Ralph and Lesley Easton

*Who taught me the value of honest work
that Jared Flagg never learned.*

Contents

Illustration Credits   ix

Foreword   xiii

Chapter 1
The Making of a Huckster   **1**
A. Introduction   1
B. Young Entrepreneur   4
C. Flagg's Dangerous Idea   14

Chapter 2
Flagg's Flats   **21**

Chapter 3
On Broadway   **37**

Chapter 4
52% Flagg   **51**
Endnote   70

Chapter 5
Flagg's Trial   **73**

Chapter 6
Victorious Appeal   **93**

Chapter 7
The Cook Case   **101**

Chapter 8
Final Years 113
A. The Crimes of Jared Flagg 113

B. Flagg's Last Scam 118

C. Epilogue 123

Selected Bibliography 129

Endnotes 131

Index 159

Illustration Credits

No.	Caption	Pg. No
1	Jared Flagg Jr. in 1910. New England Historical Society.	1
2	Jared Bradley Flagg. *Hartford Courant.*	2
3	Cornelius Vanderbilt by Jared Bradley Flagg. American Gallery.	4
4	Jim Fisk. Wikipedia.	5
5	Jay Gould. Library of Congress.	5
6	Fulton Street Fish Market. New York Public Library.	6
7	The Plaza Hotel circa 1907. Plaza Hotel.	8
8	The Singer Building, Ernest Flagg, Architect. Library of Congress.	9
9	Galbraith Patent. U.S. Patent Office.	10
10	Hayward Hand Grenade ad. New Haven *Daily Morning Journal & Courier*, April 8, 1885, at 3.	11
11	No Deposit ad. New York *Evening World*, May 9, 1892, at 6.	15
12	No Deposit ad. New York *Evening World*, May 7, 1893, at 7.	16
13	R.J. Horner & Co., Museum of the City of New York.	17
14	Jobless Men Keep Going. Wikimedia.	20
15	Jefferson St. Market Courthouse & Prison. New-York Historical Society.	21

16 Rev. Charles H. Parkhurst. Library of Congress.   22

17 Sen. Clarence Lexow. Wikipedia.   23

18 Captains Donohue and Price. New York *Tribune*, March 20, 1895, at 2.   25

19 Police Commissioner Theodore Roosevelt. Library of Congress.   26

20 19th Century Prostitutes. Unidentified.   27

21 Bartow S. Weeks. *Munsey's Magazine*, Vol. VII, July 1897.   31

22 Police Office Notice. Museum of the City of New York.   32

23 The Tombs. Wikimedia.   34

24 The Sunshine of Paradise Alley. New York. Public Library.   35

25 Oscar Hammerstein's Victoria Theater. Wikipedia.   37

26 Oscar Hammerstein I. Wikipedia.   39

27 La Boheme. Aborn Opera Co. Amazon.   40

28 Hammerstein Chorus Girls. Stuffnobodycaresabout.com.   41

29 Grand Central Palace. Wikipedia.   45

30 Charlotte Odlum Smith. *The Adirondack Almanack*, July 2, 2012.   48

31 Ernest Flagg. Library of Congress.   49

32 Wall Street District. Harvard Center for History and Economics.   52

33 The Ticker Investment Digest. The Ticker Publishing Co.   54

34 Union Pacific Stock Certificate. eBay.   54

35 Original Waldorf Astoria. Library of Congress.   56

36 Wall Street Panic of 1907. Wikipedia.   57

37 The Paterno. Wikipedia.   58

38 Charles Ponzi. Wikipedia.   59

39 Daniel N. Morgan. Treasury Department.   60

40 City Hall Post Office circa 1905. New York Times   61
    Photo Archive.

41 U.S. Marshal William Henkel. Library of Congress.   63

42 Browne's Chop House. Flickr Commons.   64

43 New York Stock Exchange ca. 1908. Wikipedia.   65

44 The Tombs—Again. Wikipedia.   66

45 Flagg's Flats. Amazon.   67

46 Madeline Russe. *Buffalo Enquirer*, Sept. 27, 1911, at 1.   68

47 U.S. District Judge E. Henry Lacombe. Wikipedia.   69

48 Hazel Murray. *Democrat and Chronicle* (Rochester,   74
    N.Y.), Sept. 29, 1911, at 1.

49 The Flagg Raid. eBay.   76

50 Consolidated Stock Exchange. Wikipedia.   77

51 Ledger. General Ledger Icons.   79

52 U.S. District Judge Learned Hand. Wikipedia.   80

53 U.S. District Judge Charles M. Hough. Open Jurist.   81

54 U.S. District Judge Frank M. Rudkin. Open Jurist.   83

55 Jared Flagg, Jr. *Genealogical Notes on the Founding of*   87
    New England.

56 Caught At Last! Greensboro, N.C., *Daily News*, Nov.   91
    22, 1914, at 2.

57 52% Flagg. Beaver Falls, Pa., *Tribune*, Jan. 9, 1915, at 95
    8.

58 U.S. Circuit Judge Alfred C. Coxe. Wikipedia.   98

59 Seal of the U.S. Court of Appeals for the Second Circuit.   100

60 Gilbert E. Roe. Library of Congress.   101

61 U.S. District Judge Augustus N. Hand. Wikipedia.   103

62 U.S. District Judge Charles M. Hough. Open Jurist.   103

63 Jared Flagg Lecture ad. *Wall Street Journal*, Dec. 5, 1916, at 5.   105

64 Receivers' Notice. *New York Times*, May 19, 1917, at 16.   107

65 Cook v. Flagg. Briefs for Appellant and Appellee.   109

66 U.S. Circuit Judge Henry Wade Rogers. Wikipedia.   111

67 U.S. District Judge Julius M. Mayer. Wikipedia.   111

68 The Crimes of Jared Flagg. Amazon.   113

69 Bartow S. Weeks. Wikipedia.   115

70 Guaranteed Profit-Participation Gold Bond Certificate. Kaufman v. Flagg Corp.   120

71 Albert F. Ottinger. Wikipedia.   121

72 Jared Bradley Flagg. *Hartford Courant*.   123

73 Montague Flagg. Find a Grave.   124

74 Charles Noël Flagg. Find a Grave.   124

75 Ernest Flagg. Library of Congress.   125

76 W. Allston Flagg. 1989 Revenues.   126

77 Louise Flagg Scribner. *Genealogical Notes on the Founding of New England*.   126

78 Rosalie Flagg Jaffray. *Genealogical Notes on the Founding of New England*.   127

Foreword

I first encountered Jared Flagg while researching my biography of Gilbert Roe, a prominent civil liberties lawyer in the first three decades of the 20th Century, who just happened to represent an investor who was swindled by Mr. Flagg. (See Chapter 7.) He was such an interesting character that I promised myself I would revisit the gentleman when the Roe book was finished.

I finished the Roe book, *Defending the Masses*, then another, *New York Times v. Sullivan*, before I could spend much time on Jared Flagg. But it was well worth the wait. Court records were hard to come by, but I am indebted to archivists at National Archives branches in Kansas City and New York City, as well as the New York City municipal records office.

I also made extensive use of the Newspaper.com and the New York Historical Society library archives, following the New York City newspapers as they followed Flagg's antics. And Flagg's own wonderful writings – self-serving and unreliable as they are – were indispensable to this book. While masterpieces of "spin," Flagg's work at least provided direction for the necessary corrective research. Jared left no "papers," but I was able to access Ernest's diaries at the Avery Architectural & Fine Arts Library at Columbia University.

So, if that's the "how" of it, what's the "why"? It is possible, I suppose, to find some higher meaning in the Jared Flagg story: a "slice of life" from the Gilded Age, a morality tale for would-be con artists, even a metaphor for a certain prominent political figure. But, frankly, I pursued the story of Jared Flagg for the fun of the pursuit. Here was a spectacularly colorful character, all but forgotten by history, whose get-rich-quick schemes were ultimately disastrous. I hope the reader has as much fun reading about them as I had researching and writing about them.

Finally, I'd like to thank architectural historian and genealogist Peter Flagg Maxson for sharing with me a few anecdotes about his least illustrious ancestor. The Flaggs are truly one of this country's outstanding families, producing artists, architects, financiers, and socialites in one generation – the same generation that produced Jared Flagg. Where so much good exists, it must have seemed churlish indeed for me to focus on the "black sheep." But Peter was generous and supportive, for which I will always be grateful.

Chapter 1

The Making of a Huckster

A. Introduction

The slight, dapper seventy-three-year-old man jumped out of his taxi at 66 Broadway and ran up the stairs to the New York City offices of the state's Attorney General. He appeared to be in good health, if somewhat agitated, his thinning gray hair parted in the middle and held in place with pomade. He almost looked like a preacher in his black frock coat and waistcoat buttoned up to his chin—except, that is, for the big cigar clenched tightly between his teeth.

Jared Flagg, Jr., in 1910

It was August 26, 1926. As he approached his destination, Jared Flagg, Jr., might have seen preparations for a ticker-tape parade the following day. The parade was to celebrate Gertrude Ederle, the nineteen-year-old Manhattanite who had become the first woman to swim the English Channel earlier that month. The parade would travel up Broadway's Canyon of Heroes,[1] right past the Manhattan Life Insurance Building where the AG's offices were located. That eighteen-story, $4-million skyscraper, just a hundred feet south of Wall Street, had recently been sold to real estate operator Frederick Brown, who resold it within weeks to Manufacturers Trust Co.[2]

None of this mattered to Flagg, who had been told that he was "wanted" for questioning by AG Albert Ottinger's Bureau for the Prevention and Punishment of Fraud.[3] On his arrival, Deputy Attorney General Keyes Winter told him that he was under investigation for the fraudulent sale of bonds in connection with a property he owned on West 68th Street. Winter had just finished questioning him when Flagg collapsed in his chair from a massive heart attack. A doctor was called, but within a few minutes, Jared Flagg, Jr., was dead.[4]

Flagg's death on the "grill," as one newspaper wag put it,[5] might have seemed an incongruous and ignominious end to a scion of one of America's most accomplished Gilded Age families. His father, Jared Bradley Flagg, a seventh-generation American, had been a celebrated portraitist, respected clergyman, successful real estate developer, and biographer.[6] Both of his older brothers, Montague and Charles Noël Flagg, were Paris-trained artists, while his younger brother, Ernest, who also studied in Paris, had become a famous architect.[7] Still younger siblings included Washington Allston Flagg, co-founder of a major stock brokerage house;[8] Louise Flagg Scribner, who married publisher Charles Scribner II;[9] and Rosalie Allston Flagg Jaffray, one of Mrs. Astor's "400" most fashionable socialites of the day.[10]

A more cynical observer, however, might say the circumstances surrounding Jared Jr.'s death were quite appropriate to his life, and wholly predictable, if not deserved. Unlike his respected father and admired siblings, Jared was a huckster, a swindler, and a pimp – sometimes all three at once. During the course of his life, he had occasion to become intimately familiar with New York City's notorious jailhouse, the Tombs. Three years after his death, a New York court characterized Flagg's bond sales as "unscrupulous."[11] His most significant achievements were setting a legal precedent against warrantless seizures,[12] by which he narrowly escaped another incarceration, and the publication of several unabashedly self-serving but enormously entertaining autobiographical narratives.[13]

Jared Flagg, Jr., and his siblings represented the eighth generation of American Flaggs, a lineage that began in 1637 when

Jared Bradley Flagg

Thomas Flegg emigrated from Norfolk, England, to Watertown, Massachusetts. Thomas's son, Gershom Flagg, a tanner at Woburn, Massachusetts, was killed in 1690. Gershom's son, John, was also a Woburn tanner, but John's son, Ebenezer, became a merchant and ship owner in Newport, Rhode Island. Ebenezer's son, Henry Collins Flagg, was a surgeon in the Continental Army; his son, also named Henry Collins, became a lawyer and editor of the *Connecticut Herald*. He also served as a state senator and Mayor of New Haven. In 1820, Henry Collins Flagg, Jr., and his wife, Martha, gave birth to Jared Bradley Flagg in New Haven.[14]

Jared Bradley had six siblings—four brothers and two sisters. Perhaps the most illustrative of the family's social status was his younger sister, Rachel Moore Flagg, whose daughter Alice—Jared Flagg, Jr.'s first cousin—married Cornelius Vanderbilt II, grandson of the famous Commodore Vanderbilt. The Vanderbilts went on to build a palace at 1 West 57th St.—said to be the largest house ever built in New York City—adjacent to the land occupied today by the Plaza Hotel. This is land that Jared Bradley would later purchase. The Vanderbilts would also build The Breakers, the palatial "cottage" at Newport, Rhode Island, which remains a landmark to this day.[15]

As a young man, Jared Bradley Flagg began his study of art in New Haven with his brother George, a student of their uncle, Washington Allston. At sixteen, Jared Bradley exhibited a portrait of his father at the National Academy of Design. He settled in Hartford, where he became prominent as a portrait painter and, in 1841, married his first wife, Sarah Robbins Montague. The following year, Sarah gave birth to a son, Montague, but Sarah died in 1844 at age 20. Jared Bradley married Louisa Hart in 1846, and Charles Noël was born in 1848. The family moved to New York City in 1849, where Jared Bradley began to study theology. Jared Flagg, Jr., was born in 1853, in New Haven, one year before Jared Bradley was ordained a deacon in the Protestant Episcopal Church. In 1855, the senior Flagg was ordained a priest and became rector of Grace Church, Brooklyn Heights—"the most aristocratic parish of Brooklyn."[16]

Jared Bradley's fourth son, Ernest, was born in 1857, and his fifth, Washington Allston, in 1860. The following year, he received a master of arts degree from Trinity College. In 1862, his first daughter, Louise, was born. Jared Bradley went on to receive his doctor of sacred theology degree from Columbia College in 1863, but Louisa's health was failing, and he resigned his position at Grace Church. Jared Bradley moved his family to St. Paul, Minnesota, where the climate was thought to be better for her. Her condition seemed to improve, and the family returned to New Haven in about a year. Daughter Rosalie was born there in 1866, but Louisa died the following year. In 1869, Jared Bradley married his third wife, Josephine Bond, and, under her influence, the family moved back to New York City.[17]

B. Young Entrepreneur

Although Jared Bradley Flagg continued to paint after the family

**Cornelius Vanderbilt
by Jared Bradley Flagg**

returned to New York City, including portraits of various members of the Vanderbilt family, his financial situation was apparently strained. The younger children were sent to live with relatives,[18] while the older children were either sent away to school—Montague and Charles studied art in Paris between 1872 and 1882—or left to their own resources. Jared Jr. recalled that his stepmother asked if he wished to continue at the Hopkins Grammar School in New Haven, which he attended from 1864–69,[19] and then go on to Yale, or if he preferred to get a job in Wall Street and someday become a speculator. "I had heard of Wall Street and longed to know more about it," Flagg wrote. "I had also heard of the Greek language and longed to know less about it; so without giving the subject consideration, I selected Wall Street."[20]

Jim Fisk   **Jay Gould**

The Flaggs had a social relationship with Frank H. Work, a multi-millionaire banker and stock broker, and a familial relationship with his wife, Ellen Wood Work, who was first cousin to Josephine Bond Flagg, young Jared's stepmother. So Jared Jr. got a clerical job in Work's Wall Street offices. "I arrived on Wall Street the day of the 'Black Friday' gold panic of 1869," Flagg wrote. "Never before had I seen men rushing about in such crazy fashion. At the time, I did not know a panic was raging—I thought it an everyday occurrence—and was not favorably impressed, in fact, was depressed and remember and will always remember *that* day."[21]

One can only guess what lessons young Flagg ultimately took from "robber baron" Jay Gould's attempt to corner the gold market. With the acquiescence of President Grant and the collaboration of financier and speculator Jim Fisk, Gould began buying gold in 1869 and drove up its price. Sensing a change of heart in the White House, Gould began secretly selling gold, even as Fisk continued to buy. At noon on Friday, September 24, 1869, the federal government dumped gold on the market and the price crashed, leaving chaos, panic and ruin in its wake.[22] That was Flagg's introduction to the world of high finance, and, while he never attained the heights of a Jay Gould or Jim Fisk, he may have absorbed something of their bravado and warped moral compass.

Flagg stayed in the Work offices for five years, keeping track of stock purchases and sales, and later claimed to have thereby acquired "an insight into the intricacies of speculation." It is not clear why he lost his job with Work, but, according to his brother Ernest, who had followed Jared Jr. to Wall Street, their father was "greatly distressed" by the news. Jared Bradley was able to scrape together $1,500 to buy Jared Jr. a partnership in a salt fish business owned by John Winans.[23] In 1874, Jared Bradley sensed something was wrong with the business, and suggested that Ernest, then 17, join the company as bookkeeper. It didn't take Ernest long to realize that the firm was insolvent and had always been so. Jared Bradley lost his investment, and his sons were out of work.

Fulton Street Fish Market

Partly to keep their father from losing even more money, the Flagg brothers tried to resurrect the salt cod part of their fish business. Jared Bradley had guaranteed the Winans company's rent and would have been liable if the building stayed empty. Jared Jr. and Ernest decided to occupy the two upper floors of the building—skinning salt codfish and packing it in 30- and 60-pound boxes—and to rent out the rest. With $25, they bought a 400-kilogram box of codfish, skinned and packed it themselves, then, with a sample in a tin box, tried to sell their product to local grocery stores. They had the fish they sold delivered c.o.d. (a pun that Ernest would later find amusing), and the deliveryman brought back the money. They earned a $5 profit for three days' work.

After two or three such efforts, the deliveryman absconded with the profits, but Jared Jr. was undeterred. The brothers bought another 5,000 kilograms of salt cod on 30 days' credit, gradually hired more than 50 workers to skin and package the product, and ran a successful business for about two years, before being undercut by their chief competitor. Ernest oversaw the production aspect of the salt fish business, while Jared Jr. handled sales. During those years, the brothers rented out the entire building and moved their operations to lofts over a wholesale grocer on Harrison Street. Jared Jr. and Ernest—who had lived on the top floor of the building—moved into rented rooms uptown. When Jared Jr. was taken ill, sales fell off, and Ernest recalled that the business seemed headed for ruin. They were saved when the grocer below them complained of the odor and gave the brothers $400 to leave. They rented the ground floor of a building on Duane Street, the business revived, and over the next year their capital grew to about $5,000.

As competition increased and profits declined, however, Jared Jr. sold his interest in the company to Ernest. Ernest expanded the business to include and then to focus exclusively on the manufacture and export of the recently invented oleomargarine. Jared may have remained involved in the export aspects of the business; immigration records show that he was in Europe during 1879.[24] In any event, Ernest did reasonably well selling to English buyers until about 1881, when the European market collapsed. Ernest could not meet his debts to creditors and his equipment was seized by the sheriff. "I had no fight left in me," he recalled later. "I was crushed and wished I was dead. I saw no hope for the future."[25]

Jared remembers the years following his employment with Frank Work a little differently. "After I left Mr. Work's office I operated for myself on Wall Street a great many years; about ten years," Flagg testified many years later. "Eight or ten years after that, I started a brokerage house, and opened an office in Exchange Court, and my brother, W.A., of Post & Flagg, one of the founders of the firm of Post & Flagg, acted as my bookkeeper in that office. He had been with Robert L. Cutting & Co. prior to taking the position as my bookkeeper and cashier."[26]

In any event, Ernest Flagg had drawn considerable criticism from his creditors, including the allegation that he wrote bad checks for goods he purchased before the bankruptcy.[27] Another report alleged that he had illegally transferred $5,000 to his father, Jared Bradley, as endorser on notes that had not yet come due.[28] Whether or not that actually occurred, Jared Bradley was able to finance a real estate venture that included both Ernest and Jared Jr. With Philip G. Hubert, they invested in cooperative apartments with considerable success, and one notable failure: the $850,000 purchase in 1882 of twelve lots on the Fifth Avenue Plaza between 58th and 59th Streets, the present location of the Plaza Hotel. The plan was to construct the Fifth Avenue Plaza Apartments, "the largest and costliest apartment house of the city."[29]

According to the *Real Estate Record & Guide*, the $1.5 million building would be twelve stories tall with fifty-two apartments. The units were to include twenty simplexes, twenty-three duplexes, and nine triplexes, with direct elevator access to the apartments. Designed by architect William A. Potter, the building was to have a façade of red brick and light sandstone, with round, conical towers at the corners and a three-story-high mansard roof, looking something like a French chateau. Later that year, however, the project's financing collapsed, allegedly because the Flaggs' "share of the benefits was to be so extravagant," and potential investors backed out.[30]

The Plaza Hotel circa 1907

Jared Jr. was also "interested with his father and several others, including Augustus Hatfield and L.L. Todd, of bucket-shop fame, in a scheme for building apartment-houses on the co-operative plan. The company failed, however, and there was a great deal of talk at the time of the slick manner in which young Flagg outwitted his associates."[31]

These real estate ventures ultimately led Ernest to study architecture in Paris. When the Vanderbilts decided to double the size of their New York City mansion, Ernest made suggestions that so impressed them that they financed his study at the École des Beaux-Arts. On his return, Ernest launched a brilliant, if controversial, career as an architect.

Jared Jr. sought to augment his income from real estate through public lectures. In 1884, for example, an advertisement appeared in the *Brooklyn Daily Eagle* for the Pavilion Summer Theater at 5th and Flatbush Avenues, touting a "Great Lecture" by Mr. Jared Flagg on the subject of "Hypocrisy." The ad called Flagg "the only rival in the lecture field" of the Hon. Robert Ingersoll, a lawyer, civil war veteran, political activist, and orator who championed the causes of abolition, freethought, and agnosticism. While tickets to Ingersoll's lectures could sell for as much as a dollar, Flagg was charging ten cents admission. The *Eagle* printed an excerpt from Flagg's talk:

The Singer Building, Ernest Flagg, Architect

> Money and its accumulation is the cause of most of the hypocrisy of this world. For money man or woman will lay down his or her life. I cannot respect a man who hoards his money. Do not understand me to say that I do not admire thrift and economy, for I do. But the true principle is to help those whose necessities require your assistance. Succor the poor and needy, and God will reward you for your pains.[32]

Inspirational, perhaps, but Flagg's actual motto might well have been "sucker the rich and comfortable, and your rewards will come that much faster."

United States Patent Office.

EDWARD A. GALBRAITH, OF BOSTON, MASSACHUSETTS.

Letters Patent No. 80,720, dated August 4, 1868.

IMPROVED COMPOUND FOR EXTINGUISHING FIRES.

The Schedule referred to in these Letters Patent and making part of the same.

Be it known that I, EDWARD A. GALBRAITH, of Boston, in the county of Suffolk, and State of Massachusetts, have invented a new and useful Improvement in Compound for Extinguishing Fires; and I do hereby declare that the following is a full and exact description thereof.

My invention has reference to a class of devices or means of extinguishing fires by the employment of a jet, streams, or shower of water impregnated with fire-subduing or extinguishing materials projected upon fire by pressure or force from a suitable vessel or machine.

Experience has shown that most fires are discovered soon after their outbreak, and if a ready means of extinguishing them is at hand, in nearly every case they could be easily extinguished with a small quantity of fire-extinguishing materials, if properly directed and applied.

The object of this invention is to devise a cheap, convenient, and ready mode of checking and subduing a fire in its early stages, by neutralizing, removing, or destroying the elements causing the combustion, and at the same time so simple and convenient that any one can apply it, and be always sure of its success.

Chemically considered, if you neutralize, remove, or destroy either of the elements which make the fire, you destroy the fire.

Water does this by saturation, when sufficiently large quantities are early applied, but this is not always at hand, and there are many objections to the use of large quantities of water.

My plan is to destroy the fire by impregnating the water with materials which neutralize or destroy one or all of the elements of the fire, and at the same time have a tendency to coat over and cover the materials on fire, and thus, by operating at its roots, effect the object, and also by use of materials and substances held in solution, which, when coming in contact with the fire, will become instantly solidified, form incrustations on the burning mass, and generate and emit gases unfavorable to combustion.

This may be effected by impregnating the water to be used, by dissolving therein salt-cake of commerce, or sal-nixon of commerce, both being the residuum of the manufacture of muriatic or nitric acid; crystallized sulphate of ammonia; bicarbonate of soda; chloride of calcium; bittern-water; chloride of magnesium; bleaching-powder; Epsom salts; bisulphate of ammonia; silicate of soda; any soluble silicate or their equivalents, which, when brought in contact with the fire, will tend to destroy it by incrustation and decomposition, and, by coming in contact with the fire, creating and generating gases unfavorable to combustion.

To carry out my invention, I use a cylinder, or other properly-constructed vessel, made in any of the known forms, with the necessary appurtenances and fixtures, and, after filling it nearly full of water, I dissolve therein two or three of the above-mentioned ingredients, but prefer the salt-cake of commerce, or sal-nixon of commerce, both of which are very cheap, and remarkably efficacious in extinguishing fire, and some one of the soluble silicates and bicarbonate of soda, with or without some of the other materials, but I do not rely upon the expansive force of the fire-destroying ingredients to furnish power to project the water thus impregnated upon the fire, but use compressed air, or gas, or a small pump for that purpose, or their equivalents, which may be introduced into or used in connection with the vessel containing them in various ways.

When the materials used are fully dissolved in the water, I force them upon the fire from the cylinder or vessel used.

I do not claim in this invention any particular form or construction of vessel, or mode of forcing the water thus impregnated, do not intend to confine myself to any particular mode of carrying out this invention; but

What I do claim, and desire to secure by Letters Patent, is—

1. A solution of salt-cake of commerce in water for extinguishing fires.

2. A solution of chloride of magnesium and silicate of soda, in combination with salt-cake of commerce, or its equivalent, for use in extinguishing fires, substantially as set forth.

3. A solution of any soluble silicate, Epsom salts, and bicarbonate of soda, in combination with salt-cake or sal-nixon, or their equivalents, for the purpose set forth.

4. A solution of chloride of calcium, any soluble silicate, and bicarbonate of soda, in combination with salt-cake of commerce, or its equivalent, for use in extinguishing fires.

EDWARD A. GALBRAITH.

Witnesses:
    SELWIN Z. BURMAN,
    ISAIAH KNOWLES, Jr.

During the years between 1884 and 1892, Jared Jr. was involved in any number of schemes to make money, legally or otherwise. In 1885, for example, Flagg became involved in manufacturing fire extinguishers. Identifying himself as the New York manager of Flagg Fire Extinguisher, Flagg claimed exclusive U.S. rights under an 1868 "Letter of Patent" filed by Edward A. Galbraith of Boston to the chemical compounds used in the extinguishers.[33] Flagg's extinguishers were of the "hand grenade" type, that is, glass bottles filled with the chemicals and hurled at the fire. When the bottles broke, the chemicals were supposed to smother the fire.[34]

Flagg seems to have made an effort to protect his interest by publishing warnings in newspapers across the country that he had commenced patent infringement lawsuits in federal district court against all other manufacturers of hand fire extinguishers. "I shall proceed against all parties manufacturing, selling, using, or having in their possession" any infringing extinguishers, he wrote. "In purchasing Hand Fire Extinguishers, be careful to see that they bear the label of the Flagg Fire Extinguisher."[35]

THE HAYWARD HAND GRENADE

Is a glass globe holding about a pint of chemical fluid which generates enormous volumes of fire-extinguishing gas when brought in contact with flame. In case of fire the Grenade is thrown in and breaks, thus liberating the liquid and creating an amount of gas in the presence of which fire cannot exist a moment.

PRICE, $10 A DOZEN.

HAYWARD HAND GRENADE FIRE EXTINGUISHER COMPANY,
407 Broadway,   New York.

Flagg's advertisements went on to list several manufacturers against whom he had filed a lawsuit: among them, the Hayward Hand Grenade Co. On April 8, the *New Haven Daily Morning Journal & Courier* carried a one-inch notice placed by an agent of Hayward, announcing that Flagg had been "indicted by the grand jury in New York for criminal libel last week."[36] There is at least some room for doubt as to the truth of Hayward's notice; the *Brooklyn Daily Eagle* had run a brief article on March 26, saying that Flagg had been arrested on a charge of criminal libel, but that further examination "revealed that the accusation was the untenable product of business rivalry" and that Flagg had been "honorably discharged."[37] The fact that Flagg's warning ads continued to appear, at least through June, suggests that nothing much came of the libel claim.[38] Nor is there evidence of any progress on his patent infringement claims.

The Flagg family spent much of the summer of 1885 in New Haven developing real estate—summer residences for themselves and for rental. Local newspaper reports show new buildings under construction by Jared Flagg, Jr., his father, and brothers Charles and Montague.[39] Increasingly, however, Flagg seems to have been spending money beyond his means. In October, Flagg lost two court cases, requiring him to pay $100.47 to the Metropolitan Job Printing Co., and $62.71 in an action on a note held by Terwilliger & Peck.[40] A few months later, Flagg was in court again, accused of absconding with building materials and furnishings from three separate companies: A.C. Chamberlain & Son, Lehigh Valley Cement Co., and New Haven Pipe Co.[41] In June 1886, David R. Brown was awarded a default judgment against Flagg for $566 plus costs.[42] Flagg was not the only family member to find himself overextended: in February 1887, New York City won a judgment from patriarch Jared Bradley Flagg for $1,239.99—the down payment on a New York City flat that the senior Flagg never delivered.[43]

A retrospective of Flagg's activities during the late 1880s and early 1890s, published by *The World* several years later, attributed to Flagg the organization of a poker club said to victimize young, inexperienced men who were induced to patronize the games. He was also involved in a theatrical agency, a beer garden, and a loan insurance company, all of which, *The World* boasted, were eventually exposed by the press. Yet another scheme, called "Flagg's Boneless Codfish," hooked a number of investors who lost all of their money when the boneless codfish never appeared on the market.[44] And in 1887, he published a book entitled, *How to Take Money Out of Wall Street*,[45] which outlined an investment scheme that would later threaten to send him to prison.

Some of Flagg's more questionable activities came to light when *The World* was sued for libel by another con artist named Champion Bissell, with whom Flagg worked during 1887 and 1888.[46] According to Bissell's complaint, *The World* published numerous false and defamatory articles about Bissell—many of which implicated Flagg as a co-conspirator—and his practice of selling worthless letters of credit, purportedly issued by a British bank, then refusing to give promised refunds to customers who found that no one would accept the letters.[47] An

August article, for example, said Flagg was working "hand-in-glove with the London Credit swindler [Bissell] and has been for the space of two years."[48]

Bissell was arrested in late July 1888, on the strength of an allegation by William J. Cooper. The arrest warrant charged Bissell with larceny in the amount of $15, and he was brought before Police Justice James T. Kilbreth. Bissell explained that the London firm of Mackie, Willis & Co. would extend a letter of credit for £100 for sixty or ninety days at 3% interest, and Bissell would charge $15 to make the arrangements. Kilbreth was skeptical, accusing Bissell of engaging in a "gigantic swindle," and sent him to the Tombs.[49]

Jared Flagg allegedly played two roles in this episode. First, according to strong implications in *The World*, Flagg posed as a Mr. Eugene Lammot, who purportedly witnessed the transaction between Cooper and Bissell. Lammot/Flagg signed an affidavit that—had it been accepted—would have absolved Bissell of any fraud.[50] Second, following a conversation with Bissell in jail, Flagg offered a *World* reporter $25 not to publish an article on the matter.[51] "There is little doubt that [Bissell] and the redoubtable Flagg are partners in 'business' and concoct their numerous confidence schemes in concert." The newspaper promised that it would keep a "weather eye" on the pair in the future.[52]

Indeed, *The World* sent a reporter around to interview Flagg in August 1888. Flagg reportedly expressed concern that he might be next to follow Bissell to the Tombs. At first, he denied that he had colluded with Bissell, but, when confronted with a letter identifying him as a phony furniture appraiser in one of Bissell's fraudulent insurance/loan schemes,[53] he admitted to working for Bissell under duress. Bissell had also denied any partnership with Flagg, but *The World* clearly thought otherwise. "[W]ith the evidence gathered by the 'World,' and which grows stronger each day, their denial will be received by the public as rather fishy."[54]

In October 1888, *The World* reported that an unnamed young man—quite possibly a *World* reporter—placed an advertisement in the paper, seeking a loan of $500.[55] Both Flagg and Bissell responded, asking him to call at their respective offices. A *World* reporter "went in his place," calling first on Bissell at 39 Broadway. Bissell reportedly offered, for $15, to arrange for a letter of credit for £100 from "that well-known London banking-house of Mackie, Willis & Co." Flagg, at 25 E. 14th St., wanted $5 to "try" to get a loan for the man, but with no guarantee. "[S]till at their old games," *The World* wrote.[56]

For the record, Bissell's libel suit came to trial in the spring of 1891; *The World's* defenses of truth and privilege prevailed. Bissell appealed, but the New York Supreme Court, General Term, affirmed the trial court, holding that "Fair and true reports of proceedings before police magistrates are within both the spirit and the letter of [a statute privileging the publication of accurate reports on 'judicial proceedings'], and their publication is thereby privileged."[57]

Looking back, in 1889, the *Evening World* took a bow for its coverage of Jared Flagg and others of his ilk:

> For swindlers and rogues of high and low degree THE WORLD has ever an open eye. It has put a stop to numberless dishonest schemes, and in many cases has turned the offenders over to justice....

> Jared Flagg, Jr., is another schemer whose methods have been exposed in THE WORLD on numerous occasions. He has always managed to keep within the pale of the law and has always retained his right name. The notoriety he has acquired through the frequent exposures has rendered his schemes practically harmless....[58]

As *The World* indicated, few of Flagg's schemes amounted to much. But one—a furniture rental business—not only brought Flagg a small fortune but became prelude to a notorious citywide scandal. This episode seemed to start innocently enough, at least as Flagg describes it, with an idea. "It is dangerous to have an idea," Flagg wrote. "There is no telling where a man with an idea may land. I once had an idea and it landed me in jail."[59]

C. Flagg's Dangerous Idea

Flagg doesn't say exactly when this "idea" struck him, but as he tells the story, it was customary for young couples and others seeking to rent apartments in the city to lease an unfurnished flat and buy their furniture on a weekly installment plan, putting 10% down as security.

Seeing the deposit as a deterrent to furniture sales, Flagg approached a furniture store owner—Jacob Baumann of J. & S. Baumann Furniture—with a proposition: Flagg would solicit customers through newspaper advertisements offering furniture at no money down. Customers would be brought to Baumann, with Flagg paying the 10% deposit up front. When Bauman received enough from weekly installments to cover the deposit, Flagg would get his money back, plus a commission on everything the store received after that. If the customer failed to pay, Flagg would lose his deposit.[60]

Flagg says he began advertising immediately, using simple, two-line, 50-cent ads, and the business seemed to prosper for about four years. By 1890, however, Flagg's enterprise began to attract competitors, including Ludwig Baumann Furniture, which had the wherewithal to take out much larger ads than he could afford.[61] The advertising wars escalated, as these ads from 1892[62] and 1893[63] suggest:

In 1893, the kind of advertising Flagg was producing cost 25 cents per line daily, and 30 cents on Sunday, so the following Sunday *World* ad probably cost around $12:

FURNITURE.

Daily, 25c. a line ; Sunday, 30c.

NO DEPOSIT

or security required in purchasing furniture from me. I represent a million-dollar Western factory. Seven mammoth warehouses in New York City packed with furniture. Keep everything. Satisfaction guaranteed.

REMEMBER

NO money required down on furniture or carpets.
NO limit placed. You may buy any amount.
NO establishment has so large an assortment.
NO firm ever sold on such easy terms before.
NO house is so lenient with worthy customers.
NO honest person is ever refused credit.
NO one can offer lower prices or better goods.
NO 10 per cent. demanded before delivery.
NO extra 10 per cent. added after the goods have been selected or security required.

TERMS:

$50 worth	$1.00 weekly		$500 worth	$5.00	weekly
75 "	1.50 "		750 "	6.00	"
100 "	2.00 "		1,000 "	7.00	"
200 "	3.00 "		3,000 "	20.00	"

JARED FLAGG, JR.,

Grand Rapids Furniture Manufacturers' Agent, 242 West 23d st. ; office open 9 A. M. to 9 P. M.
FURNITURE, carpets, bicycles, folding-beds ; $50 worth, $1 weekly. Minshall, 710 8th ave., 45th st.

Not all of Flagg's buyers were "young couples," however; he appears to have had a "wholesale" operation as well. An article in the New York *Star* in mid-June, 1890, describes a "novel and ingenious" rental scheme attributed to Jared Flagg, Jr. The "operator," presumably Flagg himself, would buy a house for $50,000, paying $200 down and giving a mortgage for the balance. The house would then be furnished at a cost of $6,000, of which only one installment of $520 would be paid. The furnished house would then be rented to a tenant who, in turn, would sublet furnished rooms at $60 to $90 per week. The operator would receive $3,000 to $4,000 a year, netting at least $1,000 profit after mortgage payments and taxes.[64]

Of course, the more business Flagg did, the more he drew down what cash he had on hand. While the income from weekly installments was steady, it was barely enough to pay for advertising in the early going. Flagg explained that the furniture companies were loath to foreclose on their customers; instead, they would accept any amount the customer could pay. Flagg began giving Baumann—and, he claimed, five other firms—ninety-day notes instead of checks for his deposits. He also talked his suppliers into accepting his notes for cash to purchase more advertising.[65] But by 1894, the competition had become too much. "And so it came to pass," Flagg wrote, "at the expiration of four years that I, who had revolutionized, for the time being, the installment business of the city, suddenly found myself swallowed up as it were, just as big fish swallow little fish."[66]

R.J. Horner & Co.

The proverbial last straw appears to have been Flagg's inability to make payments to R. J. Horner & Co., furniture dealers on W. 23rd St. In the summer of 1889, Flagg purchased some expensive goods from Horner with a down payment and a promise to pay the balance in monthly installments. According to a New York *Herald* story, the firm "delivered the furniture at an uptown flat, from which it subsequently disappeared, simultaneously with a blond woman figuring as the tenant of the premises."[67] When Horner could no longer collect payments from Flagg, the company sued and won a judgment. And when Flagg failed to pay, he was ordered back to court on January 9, 1894, for a supplementary examination. Flagg's lawyers, Johnes & Travis, had the court date adjourned until January 15.

On January 14, however, Horner received an order to show cause why the examination order should not be vacated and the judgment against Flagg annulled. To the surprise of all concerned, Flagg had obtained discharge of his debts under the "two-thirds act," a little-known provision in the New York Civil Code.[68] Under the act, a debtor could petition the court for discharge from all indebtedness by showing that he could not pay his debts in full but was willing to assign his property for the benefit of creditors. The debtor was also required to file a full list of creditors, together with a written consent to the discharge signed by one or more of the creditors whose claims represented two-thirds of the entire indebtedness.

What creditor would sign such a consent? Flagg's father, of course. Flagg claimed to have $600 in assets and $40,566 in debts, of which $32,500—more than two-thirds of his total debt—represented money due to Jared Bradley Flagg. Other creditors tried to reopen the case, but Judge Henry W. Bookstaver held in Flagg's favor. Horner's lawyer was outraged. "This is one of the most remarkable cases on record, inasmuch as it reveals the existence of an illogical and iniquitous law. Flagg has been legally purged of debt, yet this two-thirds act is practically unknown in our courts. I found only three other cases on record in the Court of Common Pleas, although the act has been in operation more than twenty years. Under this law a dishonest debtor has only to use some accommodating friend to pretend that he is a creditor to the extent of [two-thirds] of the liabilities and the man goes free."[69]

On February 16, the day after Flagg's scheduled examination, a notice was approved for publication calling on creditors to appear on April 16 to show cause why an assignment of Flagg's property should not be made, as required by the law, and Flagg be discharged.[70] Flagg's $600 worth of property included an uncollected judgment for $500 secured against a daily paper for libel and the copyright in a play, "Cyclones or

The Power of Persuasion," valued at $100. Not much to divide among the creditors.[71]

Flagg never mentioned this proceeding in his memoir. Indeed, he had a very different view. "Unfortunately," he wrote, "I was not a bankrupt. Had I at that crucial moment been stranded without a dollar how different it all might have been; how different my life; how brilliant a future I might have had. My reputation was intact; my relatives had not been humiliated and I had not been 'damned' by prison bars." From Flagg's perspective, he would not have gotten into so much trouble, but for certain "resources" that he retained. Apparently, those resources consisted of furniture, which Flagg accepted from the furniture dealers in immediate settlement of their obligation to pay him outstanding commissions, over time, on the furniture he had sold over the years.[72]

At some point during the course of Flagg's furniture enterprise, one of his suppliers, Henry Thousen & Co., experienced some financial difficulties and Flagg was forced to take his commission in furniture instead of cash. "Not wishing to have this furniture 'eat itself up' in storage," he wrote, "I furnished a flat with a view of renting it at a profit." Flagg asserted that, if he had known what would happen, he never would have gone down that road.[73] It seems, however, that Flagg turned this "accident"—his word—into a thriving side business, leasing unfurnished apartments, furnishing them, and subletting them at a profit.[74] By the time his other furniture business collapsed, Flagg had 488 fully equipped flats under sublet or on the market.

"To facilitate business," Flagg recalled, "I ran an upholstering shop, a carpet cleaning establishment, a crockery and tin-pan store, and laundry in which three thousand of my sheets were washed each week. I employed book-keepers, collectors, janitors, night watchmen, scrub women, painters, paper hangers and plumbers, by the year. Also a bed-bug gang—the only one of its kind ever organized in the United States." Flagg did more than lease these flats, he bought many of them outright. "As of May 1, 1894, I held title, as shown in the Hall of Records, to over half a million [dollars worth] of flat property, all of which has since advanced enormously in value."[75] All of Flagg's buildings were located between 15th and 58th Streets, and 8th Avenue and Lexington.

Flagg's account of his thriving business begs the question: why was he doing so well when legitimate businesses all over the country were in desperate straits? In June of 1893, the entire credit system "seized up," spawning the Panic of 1893. "Before the summer was out," the authors of *Gotham* wrote, "141 national banks had failed, and hundreds more state banks, private banks, savings banks, and loan, trust, or mortgage companies soon followed them into oblivion."

> The sharp credit contraction sent debt-ridden or cash-strapped transportation and industrial corporations over the edge. During 1893 companies crashed with terrifying frequency. By year's end nearly sixteen thousand business had gone belly-up, the worst-ever toll in U.S. history....
>
> The panic raised the curtain on a five-year depression....
>
> In New York City, layoffs commenced during the summer of 1893 and reached fearsome levels during the freezing winter months. In January 1894 Mayor Thomas F. Gilroy ordered police to make a house-to-house canvas. They found about seventy thousand unemployed, of whom about 25 percent were women.[76]

Perhaps Flagg found a way to generate cash in a credit-less economy, possibly even by finding employment for some of those hapless women. That begs yet another question: to whom was Flagg renting those flats of his...and for what purpose?

Chapter 2

Flagg's Flats

Jefferson Street Market Courthouse & Prison

In 1894, the Jefferson Street Market Courthouse dominated the southwest corner of Sixth Avenue and West 10th Street. Completed twenty years earlier, the American High Victorian Gothic structure was faced in red brick, with black brick and yellow sandstone trim, and featured a high clock/bell tower with stair-stepped windows that also served as a fire watch tower.[1] The building housed the Third Judicial District Police Court, with jurisdiction that included Madison Square, the "Tenderloin" entertainment district, and that part of West 18th Street, where several of Jared Flagg, Jr.'s apartment houses were located. On May 4, 1894, Flagg was arrested for renting out those apartments for immoral purposes.[2]

Flagg was arraigned in the Police Court on charges brought by Police Captain John J. Donohue of the 16th Precinct and was paroled pending examination, scheduled for May 18 at 2 p.m.

In March, police had arrested two of Flagg's tenants, Delia Murphy and May Andrews, charging them with keeping disorderly houses. The women were fined $50 in the Court of Special Sessions. Donohue told Flagg that he would have to evict all of his objectionable tenants and gave Flagg a list. Flagg claimed to have dispossessed all 17 of the women listed, but police later found that one of them, Pauline Hastings, still occupied her flat on April 30, and they arrested her. Several other women were also found to be continuing to occupy their apartments, and Flagg was arrested within the week.[3]

The subsequent examination revealed that Flagg rented many more flats with the same reputation as the 18th Street apartments. On May 25, Flagg was indicted by a grand jury of the Court of General Sessions, where he pleaded not guilty and was released on bail.[4]

That's how the newspapers told the story, presumably based on police sources. Flagg told a rather different story, claiming that his business was flourishing and that he would ultimately have owned all of his buildings, free and clear, "had not the police manifested a disposition to go into business with me."[5] Flagg claimed that Donohue wanted a hundred dollars a month to look the other way, a demand that Flagg refused.

Rev. Charles H. Parkhurst

"[I]f I were a person who would engage in a disreputable business, I could see some object in taking [the police] into partnership with me, but as I was not one of that kind, and was conducting a lawful business, renting flats to respectable people, I could see no object in sharing profits with them."[6]

Flagg said the last blackmail demand from Donohue and "his emissary," Officer Bernard McConville, came on May 23. The indictment came two days later, on the evidence given by these two alone.[7]

There is no direct evidence that shows conclusively which of these two ostensibly conflicting stories to believe; indeed, circumstantial evidence suggests *both* that Flagg was operating a network of brothels *and* that the police were intent upon shaking him down. The investigations of police corruption by Dr. Charles H. Parkhurst's unofficial City Vigilance

League, beginning in 1892, and the 1895 final report of the New York Senate's Lexow Committee, formed specifically to investigate the NYPD,[8] leave no room for doubt that Flagg's rental properties were likely venues for prostitution or that the police would likely have sought to extort money from Flagg for turning a blind eye to his business. The Lexow report found that houses of ill-repute and the like could be found in most of the precincts of the city, operated openly under the eyes of the police, without attempt at concealment, and known throughout the community.[9] The evidence

> establishes conclusively the fact that this variety of vice was regularly and systematically licensed by the police of the city. The system had reached such a perfection in detail that the inmates of the several houses were numbered and classified and a ratable charge placed upon each proprietor in proportion to the number of inmates, or in cases of houses of assignation the number of rooms occupied and the prices charged, reduced to a monthly rate, which was collected within a few days of the first of each month during the year.[10]

One Lexow Committee witness testified specifically as to Jared Flagg's operations during 1894. Dr. John A.B. Wilson had been pastor of the Eighteenth Street Methodist Episcopal Church since April 1892, about the same time as Dr. Parkhurst's crusade against police tolerance of vice. Wilson recounted an occasion in which he complained to Captain Donohue about flats held by Jared Flagg on 17th Street. "[Donohue] explained to me that the serious trouble was that the flats were held by Mr. Flagg who gave the police more

Sen. Clarence Lexow

trouble than any other real estate man in the city; that he would remove disreputable people from a furnished flat in one part of the city to another, and so stood in with them, and it was very hard to get evidence against them."[11]

Flagg would later characterize the summer and early fall of 1894 as a period of multiple misdemeanor arrests and indictments, multiple not-guilty pleas and bail payments, and no trial on any count. "If there is any one thing in this wide world that will make a blackmailing policeman wince it is a jury," Flagg wrote. "He recoils from a jury trial as the 'Devil would from holy water'; knowing that his methods are not popular with the people, the thought of being cross-questioned is repugnant to him."[12] Although Flagg consistently claimed that he did not know that his tenants were prostitutes, the police maintained that he visited his flats frequently, and that he was familiarly known as the "old man" by the occupants.[13]

In any event, Flagg went public with his allegation of blackmail on Sunday, September 30, 1894, when Dr. Wilson read Flagg's affidavit from the pulpit. The newspapers were obviously forewarned of the event, which was extensively covered in Monday's editions.[14] According to the affidavit, Donohue called Flagg to the police station "some months ago," before Flagg's arrest in May. "The captain closed all the doors and commenced by saying, 'You have been sadly neglected; your 18th-street flat buildings are full of prostitutes, and if you want them to remain you will have to do the square thing.'" Flagg said he dispossessed a dozen disreputable tenants, but, in a moment of weakness, declined to evict one "young girl of eighteen," who had been abandoned by a man and left without a dollar. After he explained that situation to Donohue, the girl was "dragged to jail," Flagg said.

Donohue later called at Flagg's office, Flagg asserted, and the two men went to a backroom of Kenney's restaurant on West 23rd Street. "I've got you down in black and white," Flagg claimed Donohue said there, "and you have got to 'put up.' I want $100 per month; I ought to have more." Flagg said he refused to "put up one dollar," whereupon Donohue warned him there would be "consequences." His arrest and indictment followed, he said, and he was currently free on bail. "Captain Donohue is not the only captain who entertains a prejudice against me; there are others," he said. "I control and manage 822 flats in this city, and the reason, and the only reason why [they] do not like me is because I have persistently declined to permit the police force of this city to blackmail me out of money."[15]

CAPT. J. J. DONOHUE.   CAPT. PRICE.

For his part, Donohue denied all of Flagg's allegations. In a statement published in October 2 newspapers, Donohue said that he had received evidence against "disreputable women" living in Flagg's flats in March 1894 and had warned him about them.[16] He said Flagg had promised to dispossess them, and then later gave him a list of women he evicted. "I investigated and found that in some cases the women had simply been transferred from one flat to another and the names taken from the letter box," Donohue said. "I have made about nine or ten arrests in houses for which Mr. Flagg is agent since I have been in the precinct." Donohue categorically denied that he had ever asked Flagg for money. "[H]is charges are made out of whole cloth and through spite," he said, calling Flagg's bribery allegation "an absolute lie."

The stalemate continued without resolution for the rest of the year, with arrests of prostitutes from Flagg-managed apartments occasionally showing up in the press.[17] In one instance, Flagg filed a libel suit, seeking $10,000 from a certain Captain Martens.[18] In January 1895, the police war on Flagg escalated. Flagg attributed the change in strategy to a meeting that was allegedly held in the St. James Hotel on January 15. According to Flagg, Donohue and another police captain, James K. Price from the adjacent 20th Precinct, met to reconsider the strategy for dealing with Flagg. "To keep on indicting and arresting Flagg is equivalent to sticking pins in a rhinoceros," Price allegedly said. "[N]o visible effect discernible." [19] After that meeting, Flagg said, "gangs of...thugs were employed by the police to invade my vacant flats, and smash dishes, break mirrors, and rip up with sharp knives parlor furniture, cane-seated dining chairs, bed spreads, portieres, lace curtains, carpets, rugs, mattresses and pillows."[20]

Flagg wrote that his business suffered greatly from the raids; tenants and employees left his flats in droves, and the owners of buildings that Flagg only leased abrogated their agreements. He said he appealed for relief from higher police officials, but to no avail, until John W. Goff, chief counsel to the Lexow Committee, advised him to "go over the head of District Attorney [John R.] Fellows, and ask permission to appear" before the extraordinary grand jury that had been called to investigate Lexow-related charges. Flagg recounted contacting Francis H. Leggett, a wholesale grocer who served as grand jury foreman, and won an appearance.[21]

**Police Commissioner
Theodore Roosevelt**

Grand jury testimony is secret, of course, so there is no record of Flagg's testimony, except his personal recollection. Flagg said he told the grand jury about building up his business, how disastrous it would be for him to rent to prostitutes, how police captains all over the city had conspired to blackmail him, and how he had declined to cooperate with them. Flagg said he also told the grand jury about the support he had received from Dr. Parkhurst and Theodore Roosevelt—then president of the Police Board—both of whom purportedly investigated Flagg's claims. "Every man in that room was looking straight at me," Flagg wrote, "and I could feel that they...believed me...."[22]

Indeed, they did. On March 18, 1895, the special grand jury handed up indictments against eleven current and former police officers, including Captains Donohue and Price and Patrolman Henry W. Shill, who had been a "special duty" man for Price in the 20th Precinct. One count against each of those three officers was based squarely and exclusively on Flagg's testimony: "attempting to extort money from Jared Flagg, Jr., by threatening him with arrest for renting his flats for immoral purposes unless he should pay." Both Donohue and Price were released on $2,500 bail, but suspended from their police duties.[23]

The indictments of Donohue and Price did not end the raids on Flagg's flats.[24] Nor did they keep Flagg out of court. On June 10, 1895, he was arrested, again, for renting a furnished flat for immoral purposes to a "Mrs. Batcheldor," who the newspapers said was "more commonly known as Olive Wilson or Olive Howard."[25] Flagg responded to the arrest by telling the newspapers that it was just part of "a conspiracy to ruin him." He also produced a document in which "Mrs. Batcheldor" asserted that she wanted the flat to live in with her husband, contradicting an affidavit that she made at the time of her arrest implicating Flagg. As Flagg was posting his $500 bail bond, two more of his tenants were arraigned. [26]

19th-Century Prostitutes——The Mitchell Sisters?

Flagg had no sooner been released on bond than he was arrested again on the same charge, this time based on affidavits from the Mitchell sisters, Bessie and Minnie, stating that he had rented them a flat knowing it was to be used for immoral purposes. "I want to be tried because I am innocent, and can prove it," Flagg insisted in a letter to Assistant D.A. John D. Lindsay, who had managed the grand jury. "I want to once more be able to attend to my legitimate business without being thrown into a cell as I have been twice this week. I don't ask for any mercy if I am guilty, but I want you to accord me the protection I am lawfully entitled to."[27] Flagg was indicted again on June 21, apparently on the testimony of Patrolman McConville that "scores of dissolute women" occupied Flagg's flats, but again, no trial was scheduled.[28]

There was even more bad news for Flagg. D.A. Fellows moved for the dismissal of indictments in the case of Captain Donohue, on the ground that the case was not strong enough to assure a conviction.[29] The charges against Donohue were "founded upon the testimony of a man named Jared Flagg, Jr.," Fellows told Justice Daniel P. Ingraham of the Court of Oyer and Terminer, "against whom there are now seven or eight indictments."[30] Ingraham granted the motion in late October,[31] and Donohue was reinstated the following month.[32] Indictments against Price and Shill would also be dismissed in due course.[33]

Adding insult to injury, Police Commissioner Avery D. Andrews found, after investigation, that Flagg was not being persecuted by the police department as he had alleged.[34] At the time of Flagg's trial in early 1896, Andrews would say, "Flagg's charges of police persecution were referred to me for investigation. I went very carefully into the matter and spent a great deal of time. I had the witnesses before me, as well as Mr. Flagg and the police officers. I went into every detail of the matter and satisfied myself that the charges were groundless. I made a verbal report to that effect to my colleagues. I said the police performed just the sort of duty they were being paid for, and I have no reason to change my opinion."[35]

And exactly a month later, Flagg was arrested once again, following two more raids on his West 18th Street flats, and again released on $500 bail.[36] At his arraignment, he blamed the Rev. Dr. Wilson for all his troubles. Flagg told Magistrate Robert C. Cornell that Wilson had asked him to rent three flats to three preachers for $3 a week, rather than his usual price of $8. "When I refused, the reverend doctor threw up both hands and exclaimed, 'Now I know you are a bad man and rent your houses for immoral purposes.'"[37]

In November 1895, Flagg finally got the trial he was seeking—at least, it was placed on the schedule.[38] The key witness for the prosecution, Dr. Wilson, submitted his testimony in the form of a sworn deposition on

November 9.[39] Wilson left New York in early November to reside permanently in San Francisco. According to that deposition, Wilson had sent two agents to Flagg, proposing that they be put in charge of the flats—an offer Flagg declined. Wilson then sent "respectable persons" to try to rent an apartment from Flagg, but were told that none were available. Wilson said that Flagg proposed that Wilson should become treasurer of a syndicate to take charge of some flats in the area, then occupied by "colored people," whom they would replace with white tenants. Wilson said that Flagg proposed to divide a net profit of $3,000 with him, but that he refused to have anything to do with the plan. Wilson added that he thought Flagg was actually setting a trap for him.[40]

Wilson also said he was summoned to attend a woman said to be dying in one of Flagg's flats.

> I found her in an apparently comatose state. There were two other women in the room, but they did not cover her up until I had been there for some time. I asked the name of the woman; it was given: the woman who gave it said she was her sister and that she had sent for the sick woman's husband, who was in Brooklyn. I inquired his name, and she gave me another name than that she had given for the sick woman. I asked who was the third woman, and she said she was her cousin. I knelt by the bedside and offered a short prayer and then went out. I found the janitress of the building standing in the hall and I said to her sternly: "Who are those women in there?" She said there were only two. I told her there were three. "Who are they?" I asked. She gave me another set of names, different from those they had given.
>
> The next morning in passing I called there again, and was met at the door of the apartments by the woman who had been represented as the cousin of the sick woman. She was very scantily clad and was extremely effusive. I said to her: "You had better go and make your toilet." The woman I had seen apparently dying the day before walked into the room with a wrapper on. I turned and left the place, the woman calling to me to come back. I went to the station house and reported the case to the captain. Mr. Flagg said afterwards that he had rented the flat, which was right opposite the one occupied by himself, to three bachelors and that he knew nothing of the three women.[41]

Flagg's actual trial did not get underway until February 20, 1896, with Justice Joseph E. Newburger presiding. The indictment under which Flagg was ultimately tried comprised two counts: renting flats for immoral purposes and maintaining a public nuisance. Wilson's deposition was formally read into the record, and the prosecution began calling its witnesses.[42] Bernard McConville, now identified as a detective, testified that in early May, under Donohue's orders, he went to the flats complained of to warn Flagg as to the character of his tenants. McConville said Flagg promised to evict the women, but did not, and the police raided the flats a few days later and arrested one woman. McConville testified that, in police court, Flagg offered him $50 to see that the woman went free. He testified that Donohue sent him back to Flagg a short time afterward, and that Flagg asked him:

> What does Captain Donohue want, anyway? There is money
> in this thing for both of us if he will let my tenants alone.
> There is $200 a month. We can split that, and he can have
> $100 a month. If you need pocket money any time, call on
> me, and I will give you $25.

Flagg also threatened to "make it hot" for McConville if he did not stop hassling Flagg's tenants.[43]

The following day, A.D.A. Lewis, representing the state, fainted while questioning a witness. When he recovered, he called three police officers who testified not only that Flagg rented apartments for use as brothels, but also that "disgraceful orgies were held there nightly." Another officer testified that one of the flats was used as an opium den and that its tenant did a belly dance for him. Several other policemen testified in a similar vein, and the prosecution rested.[44]

Flagg himself was the key witness for the defense. He offered evidence that, in 1894 at least, Dr. Wilson thought he was innocent. The evidence was a letter inviting Flagg to send him an affidavit declaring his innocence. As previously noted, Wilson read the affidavit from the pulpit. Flagg attributed Wilson's apparent change of heart to Flagg's refusal to contribute some furniture to charity or to give three of his friends discount rental rates. Several witnesses testified as to Flagg's good character, including both Parkhurst and Roosevelt, then Flagg was recalled for a testy cross-examination by A.D.A. Bartow S. Weeks, a former bookkeeper for one of Flagg's enterprises.[45] Flagg excerpted part of that examination for his book:

> Weeks: Well, tell us, Mr. Flagg, how many of your tenants were raided during June 1895 and how many pled guilty and were fined?
>
> Flagg (to judge): May I explain under what conditions these raids were made?
>
> Weeks: I object.
>
> Justice Newburger: Objection sustained.
>
> Flagg (to jury): Do you want to get at the truth of this matter?
>
> Weeks: I move, Your Honor, to have that remark stricken from the record.
>
> Justice Newburger (to Court Stenographer): Strike it out.
>
> Weeks: Answer my question.
>
> Justice Newburger: Answer the question.
>
> Flagg: What question?
>
> Court Stenographer (reading): How many of your tenants were raided during June 1895 and how many pleaded guilty and were fined?
>
> Flagg: McConville told them, they say, that if they would plead guilty and pay a ten dollar fine they would be discharged.

Bartow S. Weeks

> Weeks: I move, Your Honor, to have that crossed from the records.
>
> A Juror: I would like to have the facts.
>
> Flagg (to judge): May I give the facts to the jury.
>
> Weeks: I object.

Flagg: Naturally, you object.

Justice Newburger (to Flagg): Any more of this and I shall fine you for contempt.[46]

Justice Newburger ultimately allowed Flagg to elaborate on his view that the guilty pleas from his tenants were induced by the offer of leniency. He also allowed Flagg's lawyer, Charles W. Brooke, to read into the record an excerpt from Flagg's 1895 book, "How to Solve the Social Problem," regarding the law that made it a misdemeanor to rent a house for immoral purposes:

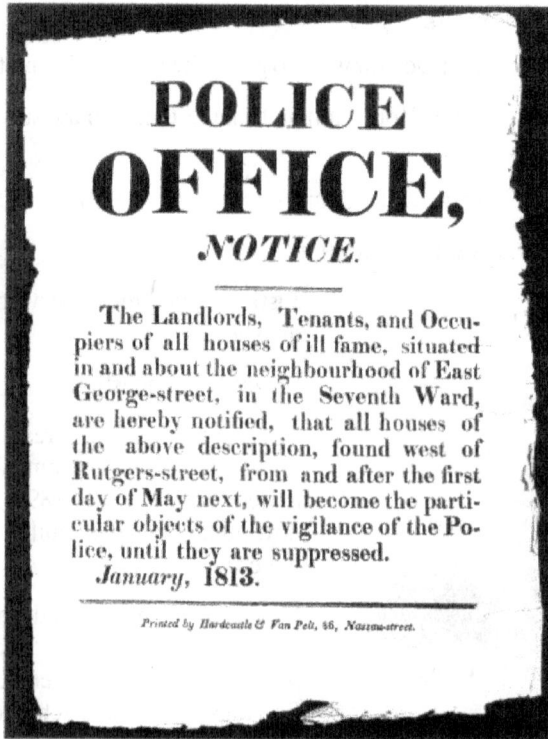

POLICE OFFICE,

NOTICE.

The Landlords, Tenants, and Occupiers of all houses of ill fame, situated in and about the neighbourhood of East George-street, in the Seventh Ward, are hereby notified, that all houses of the above description, found west of Rutgers-street, from and after the first day of May next, will become the particular objects of the vigilance of the Police, until they are suppressed.

January, 1813.

Printed by Hardcastle & Van Pelt, 86, Nassau-street.

If the law was enforced, half the real estate agents in the city would be in jail, and the other half running about town looking for bail. This law is unjust and injurious to the community when coupled with the law relating to street walkers. It aggravates the evil it is intended to suppress. Fortunately for the community the law has not been enforced for twenty-five years. The police only make a pretense of enforcing it. Every one knows that the police used the law for their financial benefit, and worked it for all it was worth for blackmail purposes.

In New-York to-day, there are five times as many immoral houses as there were three years ago. For every house closed for this crusade five disreputable flats have opened.

Out of my 688 tenants there were some immoral ones. That was sufficient to cause my arrest. All landlords are living in dread.

After Brooke read from the book, the defense rested. The court adjourned until 7 p.m., when final arguments were delivered. Brooke spoke for more than two hours, while A.D.A. Lewis took less than an hour. It was all over by 10:15 p.m.[47]

The following day, Justice Newburger charged the jury, telling them they should not convict Flagg unless they were satisfied that the alleged prostitutes rented the flats with the intent to practice their trade, that Flagg was aware of that fact, and that he knew prostitution was going on in his flats. After deliberating for more than four hours, the jury returned a verdict of guilty on the second count of the indictment, maintaining a public nuisance. Specifically, that count had charged that Flagg maintained a house in which "men and women of evil name and fame gathered, and in which there were tippling, drinking, gaming, cursing, swearing, gambling and great noise."[48] When the verdict was announced, Flagg's face turned white and he glared at the jurors. Brooke immediately asked for arrest of execution, moving that a date be set to hear argument on an application for a new trial. Hearing no objection from Lewis, Justice Newburger set March 5 for the argument. He also set bail at $5,000.[49]

Flagg's request for a new trial was actually heard on March 23, before Justice Newburger, with Brooke and A.D.A. Lindsay arguing. When the arguments were completed, the judge called Detective McConville—a key witness against Flagg—to add something about the case. Brooke erupted: "I warn Your Honor to place no faith in what that man may say in this case. He is utterly unreliable and shameless. He has declared in most profane language that he would secure the conviction of

Mr. Flagg." Justice Newburger said he didn't need Brooke's advice and would rule in a week.[50]

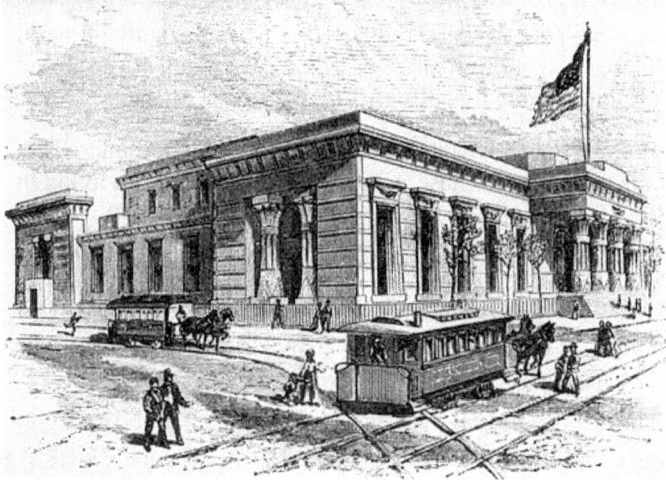

The Tombs

Justice Newburger denied Flagg's motion for a new trial and sentenced him to 30 days in jail and a $500 fine. Imposition of the sentence was stayed, pending appeal to the Supreme Court, Appellate Division. Flagg won a small procedural victory there, requiring the judgment to recite the charge of which Flagg was convicted—maintaining a public nuisance—rather than merely cite to the indictment.[51] In light of Flagg's subsequent complaints that the newspapers frequently referred to him as having been convicted of renting flats for prostitution, this win may have been some solace.[52] But he failed to serve the proper papers for his appeal, and the state's motion to dismiss the appeal was granted.[53] Flagg reported to the Tombs on December 22 to serve his sentence.[54] Flagg's lawyers continued to seek relief in the courts,[55] but to no avail.

Flagg's business deteriorated dramatically during his trial. One obvious reason was continued police harassment. In November, for example, two Flagg-managed properties on West 23rd Street came under police scrutiny. Captain George S. Chapman visited Flagg and told him that his tenants there were nearly all prostitutes. Chapman gave Flagg until December 1 to have each of his tenants sign a written pledge to use their flats only "as a place of habitation," and not for any "unlawful or immoral purpose." Any who refused to sign such a pledge in the presence of a notary would be evicted. Many of the tenants moved out, rather than sign the pledge.[56] Flagg had little choice but to "quit the flat business a bankrupt."[57]

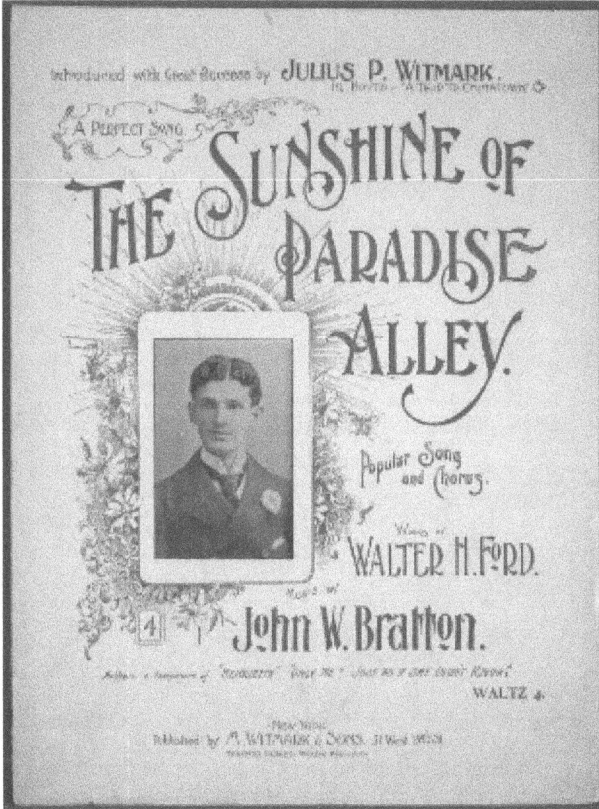

Flagg would continue to insist that the nuisance for which he was convicted had nothing whatsoever to do with brothels, but rather involved a single incident. In testimony before the court, an elderly woman complained that "some of my West 18th street tenants went on the roof one hot night in the month of July, 1895, and disturbed her by singing the popular ditty entitled, 'She is the Sunshine of Paradise Alley.'" According to Flagg, this was the only witness the jury believed.[58]

Chapter 3

On Broadway

Oscar Hammerstein's Victoria Theater

Jared Flagg, Jr., was clearly depressed when he got out of jail in March 1897. "I did not feel like admitting that I was a failure," he would write from an apartment in a building he owned at 76 Fifth Avenue, "yet I had a lurking idea that I was not what might be termed a blooming success. I felt like taking the 'rest cure,' and for a year or two I did nothing and made little or no attempt to do anything."[1] Uncharacteristically assuming the blame for his situation, Flagg said he kept largely to himself. His family did not know about his straitened circumstances, or they would have come to his rescue, he said, and he didn't have many friends.

Discounting the value of friendship in general, he did have kind words for one George D. Smith, who had stuck with him over the years. When Smith visited Flagg in 1898, a new adventure began.[2]

As Flagg relates the story, he told Smith that some of his "straight-laced" tenants probably believed what they read about him and assumed that his callers were crooked. "[O]ne old fossil, occupying an office in the floor below, INTIMATED that I was fond of women,"[3] he said, presumably because so many of his prospective tenants were young women. Smith suggested that Flagg should tell his neighbors that he was just doing business. "Why not call yourself a real-estate, or a theatrical agent," Smith reportedly said. "A theatrical agent must have callers; no callers, no business; no business, no rent."[4]

Flagg says he jumped at the suggestion, as well as Smith's offer to send any old friends who were "dramatically disposed." He tacked up a modest sign, "J. Flagg, Theatrical Agent," although he admitted he knew nothing about the business. Through Smith's efforts to drum up business, Flagg learned that the theatrical agents in New York City were organized as The Co-operative Mutual Theatrical Agents Protective Association, a guild that effectively controlled the market. He also learned that agents were paid by their clients at the rate of one-half of one week's salary, typically the second week. And he learned that theater managers usually deducted agents' commissions from performers' pay envelopes and remitted the money directly to the agents.[5]

Despite the odds against his entering the business, with or without his joining the guild, Flagg placed an advertisement in a newspaper which read, "'Attractive young women wanted for light opera chorus,' etc., etc."[6] Flagg provided no more specifics, but ads that he placed in the "Help Wanted—Females" columns over the next several years were similar:

> **MODEL WANTED—Stylish young lady; cloaks and suits; 36 bust, 43 skirt. FLAGG, 76 5th av.[7]**

> **ATTRACTIVE CHORUS GIRLS of the better class wanted; experience unnecessary; open Monday. FLAGG, 76 5th av.[8]**

> **WANTED—Young women to pose in costume for illustrators. Flagg, 76 5th Av.[9]**

Flagg said the first few respondents "did not seem sufficiently attractive in appearance for stage work," but his third advertisement brought a "living picture—Ilma Salter."[10] So attractive was the seventeen-year-old Salter, that it made no difference to Flagg whether she could sing (she could not), or dance (she could not), or act (she could not). "If we cannot put you on [the stage] we had better retire from the business."[11]

Oscar Hammerstein I

The only name Flagg knew in the entertainment management business was Oscar Hammerstein. By 1899, Hammerstein owned half a dozen theaters in New York City, most of them in what became Times Square in 1904. The Victoria Theater had just opened as a legitimate stage on the northwest corner of 42nd Street and Seventh Avenue when Flagg sent Salter there with a letter addressed to Hammerstein. The letter introduced Salter to Hammerstein and identified Flagg as a theatrical agent.[12]

As Flagg recounts Salter's adventure, she went first to the Victoria's stage door where the doorkeeper let her in and pointed to Hammerstein at work cutting a hole in the stage. Hammerstein read the letter, questioned Salter as to her theatrical skills and experience, and then sent her to M. Witmark & Sons with a letter of his own. Founded by Marcus Witmark and operated by his sons, the Witmark firm was the largest sheet music publisher in the country. It also operated a music library and talent agency, headed by one W. Ashland, who referred Salter to the Aborn Opera Co. Aborn gave Salter a contract—although for what is not clear—with rehearsals beginning within a matter of days. Salter insisted on paying Flagg, although he explained that Witmark would take half her second week's salary for the placement, and left $5 on his desk. Flagg had placed his first client.[13]

During the next three months, however, Flagg took in only $15, and three months later, dropped his price from $5 to $2. Flagg's clientele continued to grow slowly, but steadily; Ashland was placing 80% of the clients Flagg sent to him. Flagg even installed a telephone. Then one day, Flagg received a call from a Mr. Palmer of the Tams Agency, a Witmark competitor (Witmark acquired Tams in 1925), asking Flagg to send him

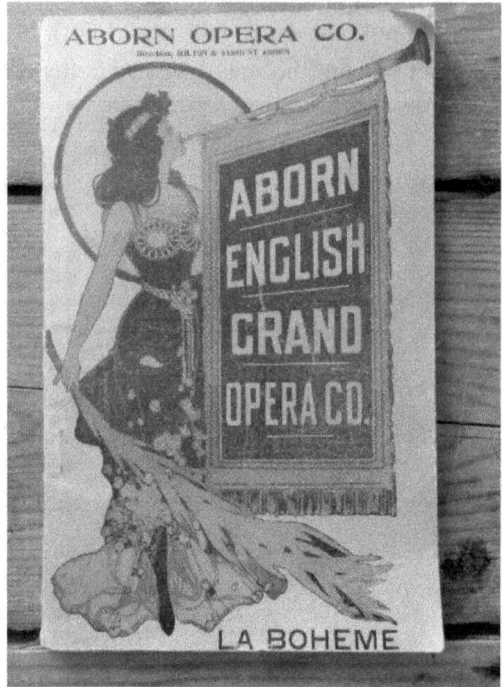

ABORN OPERA CO.

ABORN ENGLISH GRAND OPERA CO.

LA BOHEME

a few young women with good voices. The business began to prosper, doubling in year two, and again in year three. But Flagg's troubles began at the end of year four, and, as usual, he blamed them on someone else—this time, his female clients.[14]

During the four years in which Flagg promoted himself as a theatrical agent, he actually operated something like a $2-per-year registry of young women (and a few men) from which he could fulfill theatrical agencies' requests for choristers and for artists' and photographers' requests for models. While he acted as agent in some respects,[15] Flagg dealt almost exclusively with actual, licensed agents, such as Witmark and Tams. He did not deal directly with theater managers, like Hammerstein or Aborn, who requested choristers from the licensed agents. The licensed agents, of course, did not tell the theater managers where they acquired the "talent."[16]

Flagg wrote that his problems began when his clients resorted to various tricks to avoid paying agency commissions. One such trick exploited the way theater managers knew which agent to pay the commission deducted from any particular chorister's second week's pay. The women would simply line up on pay day, and the manager, his bookkeeper, and agents would walk down the line and check off the names. That system worked well enough if the women were truthful, Flagg said, but their creative use of hair dye, makeup, and stage names could confuse the agents.[17]

Hammerstein Chorus Girls ca. 1920

In other cases, the women would not visit any of the licensed agencies, but merely waited until Flagg received an order for auditions, then followed Flagg's client to the agency and, finally, to the theater. In the lineup, under both of these schemes, the women all claimed to be represented by Flagg—who did not receive commissions. Thus, there was no need for deductions from the women's pay. When the theater managers learned that Flagg only charged $2 per year, many of them began to deal directly with Flagg, bypassing the agents altogether.[18]

Needless to say, the agents were not happy about being cut out of their commissions. The Protective Association appointed a committee to meet with Flagg and urge him to join their guild. On September 9, and again on September 17, 1904, Flagg received letters from the Association inviting him to meet with them. Reasoning that adopting the agencies' business practices would effectively put him out of business, Flagg declined. What followed, at least as Flagg described it, is reminiscent of the campaign conducted against him by the police with respect to his flats. This time, he claimed, the newspapers in which Flagg was advertising received anonymous letters complaining about Flagg's business and urging the papers to decline his advertising. At the same time, police were arresting his clients—two here, three there—on the basis of rumors that Flagg was, in his words, "sending people to improper persons."[19]

On September 24, *The Sun* ran an article that could be read as confirming Flagg's charge of a rumor-mongering conspiracy against him. Or it could be read as confirming Flagg's reputation as a shady operator, especially where young women were concerned. The headline says it all:

LICENSE LAW COVERS FLAGG,

---

*whose "agency" for women
has been looked at askance,*

**He Collects $2 Now for 'Access' to Lists of
Theatrical Agents and Men Who Want
Female Models—But it Won't Prevent
His Having to Give Bond to Be Decent.**[20]

The license referred to in the headline was a license to operate an employment agency, required by the state legislature in the previous session. Responsibility for issuing such licenses fell to the newly created Department of Licenses and its commissioner, Frederick L. C. Keating. The article quotes Keating as saying that all grace periods associated with the new law had expired and that his agency would begin enforcing its requirements. *The Sun* said there were hundreds of agencies in New York that had not yet complied.

One of those agencies was Jared Flagg's, the story said, snidely identifying Flagg as having a "checkered career" who was "the son of an Episcopal clergyman and used to pose as a friend of Dr. Parkhurst." It pointed out that Flagg advertised for "stylish, dainty chorus girls of the better class," with no experience necessary. And it related the story of one woman—a Miss Evelyn Wheeler—who had paid her $2 fee, but did not get a job. "Flagg, however, appeared to take a great personal interest in her," *The Sun* claimed. "So insistent was he, in fact, that the young woman found it necessary to give him an ocular demonstration of her ability to appear to a good advantage in tights."

According to the article, when Flagg was notified that he needed a license, which meant paying a $25 fee and posting a $1,000 bond, Flagg balked. He began issuing a new receipt with the following disclaimer:

READ CAREFULLY

I am not a Theatrical Agent or an Employment Agent. I charge no cash fee or contingent fee. I accept no orders from Theatrical Managers or others. I procure no stage or posing or other engagements, and can only be of service to Young Women who are strangers in New York, or who are not acquainted with the Theatrical Agents, Illustrators and Commercial Photographers of the city.

I keep in my office an up-to-date list of the illustrators, and also a list of the Theatrical Agents, and I sell the privilege of access to these lists for a period of one year for Two Dollars.

Jared Flagg
76 Fifth Ave., New York—1904

Received from Miss _____ Two Dollars, payment in full for one year's subscription to the aforesaid lists.

When told about the new receipt, Keating said it would have no effect. "I have no desire to be arbitrary or to compel any person to take out a license whose business does not come within the scope of the law," he told *The Sun*, also noting that his department "is sure to bear heavily on the swindling employment agencies which have heretofore thrived by the thousand in this town."[21]   Apparently, Flagg threw in the towel, because three days later, *The Sun* reported that Keating had issued a license to Flagg.[22]

If Flagg caved on the license issue, he seems to have taken the offensive on other fronts. *The Sun's* notice that Flagg got his license, for example, was buried in a brief article correcting its previous reporting that Flagg had been convicted of renting flats for immoral purposes, rather than for maintaining a public nuisance, although it made clear that "public nuisance" under the law could mean a brothel, and would not likely mean a single instance of a handful of tenants singing "She is the Sunshine of Paradise Alley" too loudly at night.[23]

Flagg claims to have also received a letter from District Attorney William Travers Jerome, dated October 7, 1904, responding affirmatively to his appeal for protection, presumably from the arbitrary arrests of his clients.[24]   And, in early 1905, Flagg wrote a long letter to the business managers of New York's newspapers, explaining the wrongs done to him by the theatrical agents and pleading with them to accept his advertising. Apparently, the letter was effective; Flagg wrote that "every manager of every paper who had been constrained to reject my advertisements immediately inserted them."[25] Still, Flagg failed to win the respect of the agencies that lost money every time Flagg placed a chorus girl directly in a theater.

On January 6, 1905, a meeting was announced for a week later to discuss enforcement of the License Law—particularly as it applied to theatrical productions. Flagg wrote that the meeting was sponsored by the Theatrical Agencies Protective Association;[26] contemporaneous newspaper accounts, however, say the meeting was called by the Actors' National Protective Union of America.[27] The actors sought protection from unscrupulous "employment agencies" that lured female applicants into prostitution, and male applicants into hard labor on the Panama Canal.[28] Such practices would also cut into the legitimate agencies' profits by diverting prospective clientele to more attractive, but ultimately fraudulent offers. Indeed, one of the charges leveled against Flagg in the agencies' alleged rumor campaign was that his agency was merely a cover for recruiting prostitutes.

Grand Central Palace, New York,

Nevertheless, it is hard to imagine that the agents sponsored this conference as Flagg asserted. Even the legitimate agents were wary of the law, which was squarely aimed at protecting their clients, and they lobbied against what they called treating actors like laborers. In any event, the meeting—which was held on January 13 at the Grand Central Palace at 43rd Street and Lexington Avenue—had a decidedly unionist flavor. "A lot of men and women who are on the stage won't join a union because they think it lowers their dignity," said union president Joseph M. Lawrence. "[B]ut many a laboring man and woman is better off than are the members of our calling."[29]

Licensing Commissioner Keating, the featured speaker, insisted that the law would be enforced, despite opposition from the theatrical agents. "In the course of the next few weeks," Keating said, "we will arrest a number of agents who are not complying with the law." Keating said he expected to put some 400 to 500 of the "hat book" brand of agents out of business.[30] "In a few weeks, maybe days, we shall place under arrest several theatrical agents," Keating said. "District Attorney Jerome and I will pick out our own men and we shall make a case for the people and not for the agents."[31]

Flagg seems to have taken that warning personally. "[Keating] told the agents how much respect he had for them and how little he had

for any man who would advertise to place young women on the stage,"
Flagg wrote. "He refrained from mentioning my name, but every one in
the hall knew to whom he referred."[32] Keating proved to be a man of his
word. The newspapers reported any number of license revocations,[33] even
arrests,[34] and Flagg claimed an inspector came to his office the day after
Keating's speech, with a stenographer to take down a list of Flagg's
hundreds of clients. Flagg accused Keating of acquiring his client list in
order to find someone who would enter a complaint against him.
Apparently, no such client was found. "And, after wasting a great deal of
the city's money," Flagg wrote, "Keating gave it up as a bad job."

Meanwhile, Flagg's business continued to grow, helped along by
a circular he distributed entitled, "Advice to Those Who Denounce the
Stage," aimed at persuading parents to allow their daughters pursue a
career as a chorus girl. A sample of the pitch: "If you wish your daughter
to feel that life is worth living you will permit her to be occupied in some
pursuit which engrosses her mind.... Many of the most refined and
cultured young women (and with the consent of their parents) are now
adopting the stage as a means of livelihood."[35] He also began telling his
clients that he would "hold responsible" any theater manager who
employed one of them for rehearsals—for which she was not paid—and
then fired her. He distributed another circular authorizing any clients in
that situation to contact his lawyer, "who would prosecute their claims and
pay over to them the full amount recovered without deducting therefrom
one dollar for legal fees or disbursements."[36] Flagg boasted that he never
lost a case; the theaters settled all claims. But he admitted that he had now
alienated the theater managers as well as the agents.[37] In the end, he lost
his license, the result, he insisted, of the two combining against him.

By March 1906, when his latest downfall began, Flagg claimed to
have cornered the market for chorus girls. "[E]veryone said I had them
all," he bragged, "and there was truth in it." Flagg had begun celebrating
his success by throwing a five o'clock tea one afternoon each week for his
clients. "At each affair a different hostess presided," he said, "but
chaperoned by her mother."[38] It seemed that the only negative was his loss
of George Smith to romance. "I felt sorry for him, sorry he was not on
board," Flagg wrote, "that his fiancée had turned his head, that she had

persuaded him to eschew theatricals, settle down and live the simple life."[39]

But Flagg had made many enemies among the theatrical agents and theater managers, particularly one agent named Webster Cullison, who resented Flagg's policy of favoring direct placement with theater managers over referral to agents. On March 25, 1906, Cullison hosted a meeting of fifteen agents to discuss "that man Flagg." Flagg tried to get his hands on the minutes of that meeting in order to pursue a criminal conspiracy action, as did District Attorney Jerome, but those minutes never materialized. Flagg later wrote he "assumed" that the agents discussed ways to challenge the renewal of his license when his current license expired on May 1, 1906, based on his earlier conviction. It may well have been an exercise in perfect hindsight, but he also "assumed" they discussed bringing that challenge, not in their own names, but using the Woman's Municipal League and the Woman's Rescue League as proxy.[40]

On April 3, 1906, Laurence G. Goodhart, who had represented theatrical agents, filed an objection to the renewal of Flagg's license on behalf of the Woman's Rescue League with the new Licensing Commissioner, John N. Bogart. Bogart scheduled a hearing for April 28. On the appointed date, Goodhart appeared along with Helen Arthur for the Woman's Municipal League and former Licensing Commissioner Keating for the Theater Manager's Association. Bogart began by reading Goodhart's letter of protest, one sentence of which charged that Flagg had been imprisoned for two years for "decoying" young girls into brothels. Flagg interrupted the reading to denounce the charge, denying, correctly, that he had never been in state prison. Repeating his usual explanation for the 1896 misdemeanor conviction, and the support he received then from Parkhurst and Roosevelt, Flagg asked the reporters present not to print the false allegation lest it destroy his current business. "I have 7,000 young ladies who pay $2 each year for registering with me to get employment in the theatrical profession and with artists," he said. "To publish untruly that I have been in state prison would ruin all that business."[41]

The defense case consisted primarily of attacking the legitimacy of the witnesses against him. When Flagg's lawyer, H.D. Mildeberger, questioned Charlotte Smith, who identified herself as president of the National and International Woman's Rescue League, she seemed to have a difficult time establishing League's existence. Goodhart then asserted that Smith was testifying as a private

Charlotte Odlum Smith

individual, not on behalf of any organization, and Bogart obligingly cut off any more questions about the League. Flagg would later write that Smith was merely a con artist. Helen Arthur, head of the Woman's Municipal League's research department, retracted in writing everything she had said against Flagg previously, he wrote.[42]

Bogart asked Goodhart for proof that Flagg had been imprisoned and adjourned the hearing until May 2, on Goodhart's promise to produce it then.[43] At that time, Keating submitted court records from April 6, 1896, showing that Flagg had been convicted of keeping a disorderly house. Bogart accepted those records as accurate—even though they had long since been corrected—and, on May 2, 1906, denied Flagg's renewal application.[44] Flagg instructed his lawyer to appeal the case by petitioning the Appellate Division of the New York Supreme Court to review Bogart's decision.[45] During his preparation for the appeal, however, Bogart learned that his "certified" copy of Flagg's earlier court record was wrong and, on July 7, he informed Flagg that he had annulled his earlier decision and scheduled a new hearing for July 23.[46]

Flagg was not looking for a new hearing, and won a temporary injunction in the Supreme Court against further proceedings.[47] After many delays and a bitter legal fight, that injunction was vacated by Justice V.J. Dowling, and Flagg was ordered to appear before Bogart once again. The hearings dragged on for several months, when Flagg received a stunning letter from his brother Ernest:

> If I were you I would waste no more time or money in trying to procure a license. It is not worth it, and I wish you would cut loose from this whole unsavory mess and turn your attention to something that has a future and is worthy of you and your bringing up. I am sure if you look around you will find a profitable opening in some direction.

> You may think your past record a handicap, but I doubt if it will prove as much of a one as you imagine. If you will take my advice, I will stand behind you and will show my confidence by not limiting you in time or amount. When you want money ask for it and I will send it to you.[48]

Flagg withdrew his application, which Bogart acknowledged on February 6, 1907.[49]

Ernest Flagg

In his retelling of this episode in *Flagg's Flats*, Flagg insisted he never in his life "advertised for 'young girls to act as artists' models," adding that no newspaper would accept an advertisement of this nature.[50] No doubt Flagg would distinguish the ad that he did run in the *Times*:

"WANTED—Young women to pose in costume for illustrators."[51] He also reprinted many of the headlines concerning the license renewal proceeding that were untrue:

FLAGG SERVED A SENTENCE OF TWO YEARS IN AUBURN STATE'S PRISON FOR THE CRIME OF DECOYING YOUNG GIRLS TO HOUSES OF ILL-REPUTE[52]

Or unproven:

FLAGG DENIED A LICENSE. IT HAS BEEN INTIMATED THAT HIS AGENCY WAS IN REALITY A FEEDER FOR DISORDERLY HOUSES[53]

Flagg also said he filed libel lawsuits against Edward R. Carroll, chief clerk of the Court of General Sessions, and his assistant, William Hanna, for falsifying the "certified" record of Flagg's 1896 conviction.[54] He does not say he withdrew those lawsuits, but there is no record of a reported decision.

Chapter 4

52% Flagg

No sooner had Flagg dropped his bid to renew his theatrical agent's license, but he launched his newest venture from his office on the third floor of the building at 76 Fifth Avenue. This time, Flagg hoped to parlay his 1887 book, "How to Take Money from the Stock Market," into an actual investment firm. On April 5, 1907, Flagg received from the printer several hundred copies of his new pamphlet, labeled "Full Particulars," which he promptly shared with the press.[1]

Both the *Times* and the *Sun* carried stories written with tongues firmly in cheeks, but the *Times*'s banked headlines bear repeating:

FLAGG'S NEW GRAFT
'HAS MILLIONS IN IT'

———

Ex-Convict Starts a Highly
Original Wall Street In-
Vestment Bureau

———

YOU CAN'T LOSE, SAYS HE

———

It's Only Necessary to Put Perfect
Confidence in Flagg to Get
Rich Quick[2]

———

Still, both newspapers carried a long and detailed description of Flagg's scheme, and neither offered evidence that it wouldn't work. Flagg, of course, never expressed a single doubt about his scheme's efficacy or propriety, and he recalled it almost poetically years later:

> Twenty-four years ago—1887—impress the date upon your mind—twenty-four years ago; it was in the month of February, and it was cold, biting cold, ears were tingling and overcoats were buttoned up tightly. It was early in the evening. Lights were beginning to flicker in the store windows, when from out of the crowded thoroughfare (lower Broadway) a young man turned into Ann Street, and walked as a man walks when he knows where he is going and is in a hurry.
>
> His hands were jammed deep into his outside coat pockets; and if anyone had taken the trouble to notice, he would have seen projecting slightly from one of these pockets a roll of yellow paper; and if he could have looked inside of the same pocket he would have seen a hand clutching tightly to it. It was not because the young man was afraid any person intended to grab the paper that he held it so tightly. He knew no one wanted it, but he did not want to lose it. It meant something to him; it represented thought and study; it had cost him days, weeks, months and years of labor.
>
> It was a manuscript.
>
> And it was I—Jared Flagg—with my manuscript, who turned the corner that cold winter evening, twenty-four years ago, on my way to the old-time publishing house of Dick & Fitzgerald, 18 Ann Street, New York City.[3]

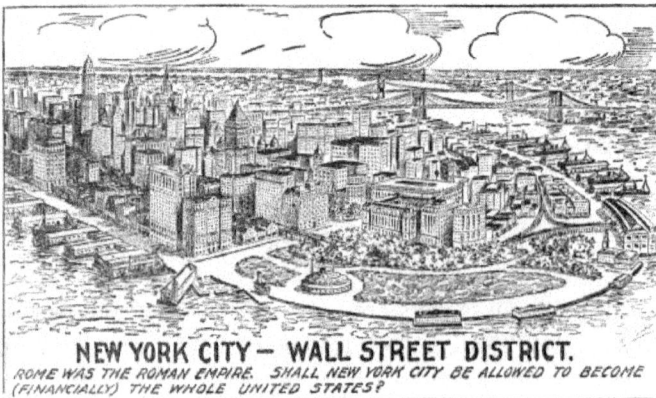

NEW YORK CITY — WALL STREET DISTRICT.
ROME WAS THE ROMAN EMPIRE. SHALL NEW YORK CITY BE ALLOWED TO BECOME (FINANCIALLY) THE WHOLE UNITED STATES?

Dick & Fitzgerald did indeed publish the book, which was well-remembered by future Wall Street commentators. "There was another book, *How to Take Money Out of Wall Street*,[4] by Jared Flagg," wrote Richard D. Wyckoff, "which consisted of a plan for being long of certain small units of stock and short of certain others simultaneously, so that whichever way the market went a profit would be secured on some of the lots, and, it was hoped, all of them eventually. Incidentally, I understand that Mr. Flagg has since gotten into numerous difficulties while attempting the actual demonstration of his theories."[5] Indeed he did, but not until after he had become wildly successful.

Flagg attributed his scheme to his one-time Wall Street employer, Frank Work, for whom he kept the purchase and sales records from age fourteen to nineteen. By studying these books, Flagg claimed, he learned the intricacies of the "scale" method of speculating.[6] The principle seemed simple: when the price of a stock rises 1%, sell; when it falls 1%, buy more. Since over time, stocks will advance and decline to the same extent, so the theory goes, the investor will only realize profits, and never experience a loss.[7]

What made Flagg's proposed operation different from other "scale" systems in the past, he told reporters, is that he was willing to take on even very small investors. Flagg said he would bundle small numbers of shares in order to meet Exchange minimums and avoid excessive charges. Flagg also assured skeptical reporters that he was able to monitor all of the market fluctuations required to know when each stock he trades goes up or down a point through his brokers on the exchange floor. The *Sun* reporter noted pointedly that Flagg had no ticker in his office.[8]

Flagg assured the reporters that an investor could make a fortune following his scheme. "I tell you confidentially," he told the *Sun*, "it is the same principle which made 'Al' Pettybone [sic], the Los Angeles gambler, a millionaire. 'Al,' you know, made his money by multiplying his bets. He played the red or black cards, and when he lost, he increased the bet next time. If he won, the next time he took a rake-off and resumed the original-size bet. See?"

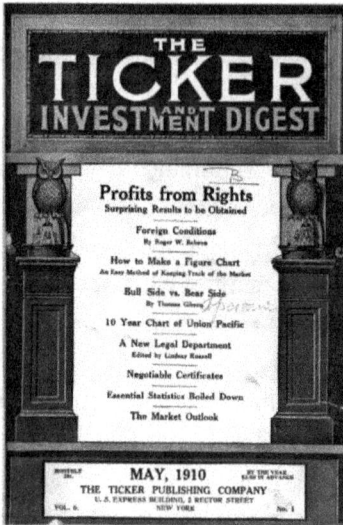

Although none of the reporters on that first day could explain why the system worked—or not—a prominent investment magazine could and did, a few years later. "The weak point in any scale proposition is usually the man who gives the orders," *The Ticker* wrote. "Out of the thousands of people who endeavor to make money by trading on a scale we have never known anyone to make a big bunch of money and get away with it. Everyone who operates this way will hit it at times, but it is not what you make so much as what you keep, that enables you to retire in peace to your place in the country."

With specific reference to Flagg, the magazine pointed out that, "[e]very once in a while some one pops up with a brand new idea on scale trading, and on paper it certainly looks good, but upon boiling the plan down and trying it out over a bad period, we almost invariably strike a snag.

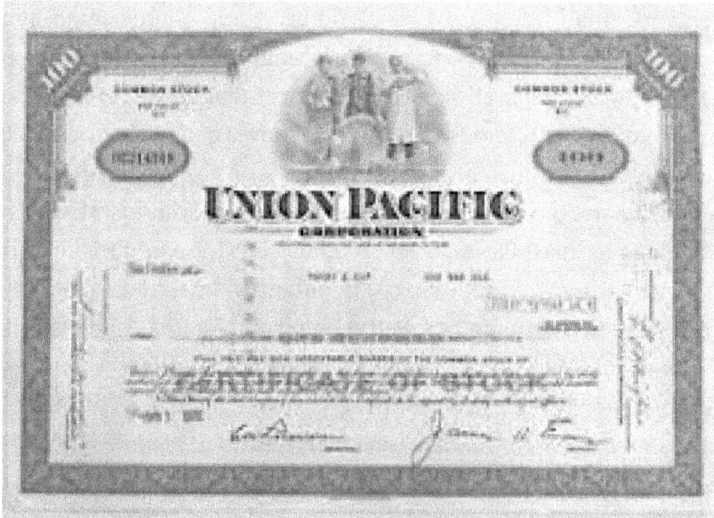

There is one little game of playing on a scale which would turn in several points a week if somebody would guarantee to keep Reading

[Railroad] within a range of, say, 5 points for a period of six months; but let the stock break out of this range on one of its phenomenal runs and the result will be that Mr. Scale-trader goes up in the air, because he either has not money enough to stand the racket, or his nerve gives out at the critical point.

> When we were all small boys there was a party by the name of Flagg who wrote a book, "How to Take Money out of Wall Street." Flagg's idea was full of scales, which may have been the reason why it sounded fishy. He figured that a stock which rose 5 points was bound to react (i.e., fall), say 2½ sooner or later, so he got on both sides of the market, buying St. Paul and selling Union Pacific or some other stock simultaneously. In fact, he never did buy something unless he sold something else at the same time, and whenever he could secure a point profit he grabbed it.

> He illustrated the idea in this way: "You have often seen a boat stranded on the beach at low tide. Well, that boat don't stay there, because the next high tide lifts it a little and enables it to float. It is just like this with stocks which we buy and sell. Sooner or later, no matter how high they go or how low they go, they come back and we get our profit."

> Mr. Flagg probably forgot that stocks like Lackawanna, Great Northern, etc., are apt to sell very high, cut melons (i.e., take profits), and then go up some more. In other words, some of the boats which you may try to float under the Flagg method may be stranded so high that nothing will ever float them again.[9]

In early 1907, however, it mattered very little whether Flagg's scheme could work or not. He simply didn't have the capital he needed to run the scheme. As a result, Flagg put up with a "small royalty" while he tried to raise money, first, from rich capitalists, then, toward the end of the year, from personal friends. Armed with charts and statistics dating back thirty years, Flagg claimed to have persuaded his friends that they could take money out of Wall Street using his method. The Jared Flagg Company was born in early January, 1908.[10] Flagg became general partner, with Robert R. Crook, Thomas L. Farrar, Henry A. Jackson, Edward L. Schiller, and James T. Schock as special partners.[11]

Original Waldorf-Astoria Hotel

In an effort to look prosperous, Flagg wrote, the firm promptly moved to more luxurious quarters in the Century Building at 1 West 34th Street, at Fifth Avenue, opposite the Waldorf-Astoria Hotel. "[T]he marble front looked inviting and the entrance was faultless.... [W]e had letter files, telephones, tickers, private wires, everything—everything but business." A small classified advertisement in the Rochester, N.Y., *Democrat and Chronicle*, on January 12, read: "If you wish to make small steady income in Wall St., without risk, with moderate capital, write now for full particulars."[12] And on February 5, the Meriden, Conn., *Daily Journal*, carried a similar ad.[13] But there was still no business, and with the rent coming due, the partnership was dissolved and Flagg moved back to his combination office and bedroom at 76 Fifth Avenue for $10 a month,[14] with Crook, Farrar, Jackson, and Shock becoming mangers, and Schiller continuing as Flagg's employee.[15]

In retrospect, it is not surprising that Flagg's initial foray into the stock market failed. In October 1907, just as Flagg was casting about for financing, the stock market fell almost 50% from its previous year peak in the Panic of 1907. A number of New York City banks were saved from failure only by the intervention of J.P. Morgan. The recession that followed lasted until June 1908, when a recovery began. One of the major causes of the panic was the unregulated speculation on the price of securities by people who did not own them, but rather placed bets on their rise or fall through so-called "bucket shops," which were not outlawed until 1908.[16]

Wall Street Panic of 1907

Flagg adamantly rejected any comparison. "This business is strictly on the level," he had told reporters, "and there is no bucket shop or bunco method about it." He also tried to persuade potential customers that panics like the one just experienced were no problem. "Panics and raids and slumps are a godsend to us," his prospectus read. "[W]e are just as much pleased to see the market go down as up. So long as it keeps going we are satisfied and the profits will roll up quickly...."[17] As the panic receded, slowly but surely the customers came. By January 1, 1909, Flagg had "'turned' our first $100,000 of working capital."[18]

As Flagg put it, "Ten shares were bought, and although I encountered a few obstacles, the business prospered—up, up, up. One thousand, one hundred thousand, a million dollars and over!"[19] Well before the end of that first year, Flagg proclaimed, "all seven rooms on the top floor of 76 Fifth Avenue were occupied by my clerks."[20] Indeed, an article in the *Evening World*, a particular nemesis of Flagg's, described the offices in some detail:

> A modest sign at the entrance to the Fifth Avenue building directs anyone interested to "Jared Flagg, Studio." An elevator in the rear of the building takes one to the top floor.

All the rooms on this floor are at present being used by Mr. Flagg. The front room has the appearance of a manager's office in a small vaudeville theatre. Photographs of actresses in scant costumes over whose autographs are such affectionate inscriptions as "To my dear Jared," adorn the wall. The room has a musty odor and serves as the "reception room."

There are other rooms between the front and the rear, but it is not until the back room is reached that any one inquiring into the alluring scheme is afforded the real information. That is the sanctum of the great promoter. A stock ticker, market charts and other Wall Street paraphernalia are some of the furnishings.[21]

The Paterno

The *World*'s article concluded with recapitulation of Flagg's previous conviction and other scams, but, as he put it, the adverse publicity he received "produced no more effect on my customers (and I had a few) than water on a duck's back. One customer brought in another...."[22] In 1909, Flagg moved his offices to the eleventh floor in the Tilden Building at 105 West 40th Street, and his residence to the Paterno Apartments at Riverside Drive and 115th Street. Business continued to boom through 1910. "To turn half a million dollars' worth of stock in a day was nothing extraordinary," Flagg wrote.[23]

By October 1910, newspaper articles about Flagg's operations began referring to a guarantee of 52% return on investment for investors in Flagg's scheme. "Jared Flagg is the latest get-rich-quick schemer to get in trouble," began one of them.

He has a handsome suite of offices in the Tilden Building in New York, with a big force of assistants, and was able to gather in $500,000 from credulous investors on the promise of 52 per cent. interest or returns per annum. For three years Mr. Flagg has paid his clients one per cent. a week, less the quarter of one per cent. he charges as a commission, ostensibly for buying stock, and another quarter of one per cent. for selling. The first investment of $100 in stocks is always successful. After that, well, you can guess the rest....

Little sympathy can be extended to the get-rich-quick investors, for no reputable brokerage or commission house or agents will promise the impossible, and when glittering prospectuses and promises are made by the promoters, it behooves people with hard-earned savings to exercise care and to steer clear of the traps laid for the credulous.[24]

Charles Ponzi

The accusation, albeit by implication, was that Flagg was paying his investors one percent per week, not from the proceeds of stock sales, but from the investment of new customers—a business method that would come to be known as a Ponzi scheme, after Charles Ponzi, who perfected the scam about a decade later.[25] Of course, Flagg denied all. "I have been falsely accused," he wrote. "I have been wronged—*terribly* wronged. They do not claim that I broke open a safe, but they claim that which is, if true, equally reprehensible, viz.:

That I, in order to rob people gave out or represented that 52 per cent. a year could be made on money. Did I ever say such a thing? Can any person on earth show me where I have ever written such a thing?

But this is what I did say—that the profits on transactions actually closed had averaged 52 per cent. a year on the margin. By using the word closed, I mean that if a stock has been purchased at 40 and sold at 42, it was closed—ended for all time; and on such transactions—"closed transactions"—I have said that the profits happened— *happened* to average one per cent. a week—52 per cent. a year on the margin—*not on the actual money involved, but on the margin;* and I have invariably explained the meaning of the word margin to those unfamiliar with its meaning, also the word happened.

These profits, derived from closed transactions, happened to average 52 per cent. per annum on the margin my customers had placed with me. They might in the future happen to amount to much more or to much less. We might approximate, but at best, it would only be a guess.[26]

Daniel N. Morgan

To reassure potential customers, Flagg enlisted the support of Daniel N. Morgan, former Treasurer of the United States in the Cleveland Administration, who was one of Flagg's early investors and featured as a reference in Flagg's promotional literature. "I know Mr. Flagg," Morgan told one reporter, "and in my judgment he is perfectly worthy of the trust imposed in him. He comes of a fine Connecticut family, and is a business man of integrity.

His concern is a legitimate business enterprise just the same as any other brokerage business. The attacks upon Mr. Flagg are based upon an old trouble he had with Tammany Hall. At that time such men as ex-President Roosevelt and Dr. Parkhurst were witnesses for him. I see no reason for the slightest worry on the part of investors in his enterprise.[27]

Morgan—who had as much as $200,000 invested with Flagg—was primarily involved in gaining customers' confidence. New prospects were often shown a dollar bill bearing Morgan's signature, one of which was framed and hung in Flagg's office, and were invited to contact him directly for his endorsement. An autographed photograph of Morgan also hung in Flagg's office was signed:

16 Fifth Avenue, New York

For Mr. Jared Flagg,

Written with the special signing pen used by D.N. Morgan when United States Treasurer from June 1, 1893, to July 1, 1897. More than a thousand million dollars in value of Treasury warrants were signed with it.

New York City, June 17, 1907.[28]

Nothing seems to have come of the spate of attacks on Flagg's "business" through the fall of 1910. In 1911, he said, "the business of its own momentum forged ahead even faster. I now had eighty bookkeepers and over seven hundred customers who had made and withdrawn from me in profits almost three quarters of a million dollars."[29] Indeed, Flagg changed his business model in mid-year, sending all of his customers the following message on July 1, 1911.

> In order to simplify, and so expedite the work in my bookkeeping department, I have decided, until further notice, to remit each week, on closed transactions, a check in even dollars, based on the weekly average profit made by my customers, on closed transactions during the past three and a half years. At the expiration of each fiscal year the difference whatever it may be, will be adjusted. Any customer who objects to this change can, by notifying me, receive his checks on the old basis.[30]

City Hall Post Office ca. 1905

That change may have attracted heightened government scrutiny, along with a miscue or two by Flagg himself. During the summer, one of

Flagg's "investors," a woman named Lillian Gibbs Keyes of Westfield, N.Y., called on Chief Post Office Inspector Warren W. Dickson to reassure him that Flagg's business was both successful and legitimate. Her visit was probably instigated by Flagg, possibly in response to a real or imagined complaint. In any case, it appeared to have prompted Dickson to investigate further. Soon after the investigation began, another Flagg associate, F. Tennyson Neely, a former publisher and bookseller, called on Dickson to ask whether there was anything "shady" about Flagg so he could warn other customers he had taken to Flagg. A few weeks later, however, Neely returned to Dickson's office threatening to expose him as a blackmailer. Dickson brushed Neely off, but had him shadowed by detectives. They reported that Neely had informed Flagg that the post office inspectors and Department of Justice had been "fixed."[31]

On August 1, Consolidated Exchange President Robert M. Jarvis issued an order prohibiting brokers from taking business from Flagg. Although Flagg was not a member of either the New York or the Consolidated Stock Exchanges, he had been using three brokerage firms to place his orders: Leavitt & Grant, which employed Flagg manager Henry Jackson, Blair Brothers, and McDonald & Co. Flagg obtained an injunction blocking Jarvis's orders, and continued a "desultory" business with the Consolidated Exchange.[32]

In any event, Flagg's business soon came to a screeching halt. Post Office Inspector Elmer L. Kincaid filed a formal complaint, charging that, on September 9, 1911, Flagg had sent fraudulent letters through the mail to a Pennsylvania woman, Mrs. Bertha L. Bentley, which represented that Flagg would invest her money on the exchanges at "astounding" returns.[33] This representation was false, the complaint said, alleging that there were no transactions on the exchanges.[34] In the end, postal authorities decided that the only way Flagg could guarantee such large dividends was through an illegal scheme.[35]

Flagg would later call Bentley a "nice accommodating woman," from Kincaid's hometown of Corry, Pa., whom Kincaid had known all his life. "She was willing, although she did not know me—had never seen me—had never placed a dollar of her money with me—had never proffered any—was never asked to put up a dollar with me—she was willing to accommodate the young, aspiring assistant Post Office inspector—Kincaid—she, this respected woman, was willing to raise her right hand, and close her eyes, and solemnly swear before Almighty God—that I, a man who had never wronged her, '*intended*' to rob her."[36]

On the strength of that complaint, Flagg wrote, "a lawless gang of men, 'armed to the teeth,' swooped down and wrecked my office and kidnapped me."[37] It was Saturday, September 23, 1911, after the exchanges closed at noon. Most of his bookkeepers had left for the day. Flagg was sitting at a long narrow table in the inner office, taking one last look at the orders for the following week, which he was about to mail to his brokers. In the outer office, a group of friends and "customers," whom Flagg had invited to his weekly celebratory luncheon at the Café des Beaux Arts at 40th Street and Sixth Avenue, waited for him to finish. Suddenly, he heard a noise and, looking up, saw a man blurt out, "You are under arrest. Don't move!"

U.S. Marshal William Henkel (left)

"The next moment and the place was alive with armed detectives," Flagg wrote, noting that two officers were stationed at each entrance to the Tilden Building, two more in front of his large, open safes, which officers said Flagg had tried unsuccessfully to close, and throughout his seven-room suite. Flagg tried to telephone his brother, anticipating the need for bail, but he was "pounced upon" by the police officers and federal postal inspectors who occupied the 15- by 25-foot room. "What's the matter with you?" one reportedly shouted. "Are you looking for trouble?" It was later learned that U.S. Marshal William Henkel and ten police officers led the raid, along with a number of post office inspectors under Inspector Kincaid.[38]

**Browne's Chop House
(double pediment facing trolley)**

Flagg claims to have gained the confidence of his invaders and, incredibly, taken everyone to lunch at Browne's Chop House. After lunch, they all went by taxicab to the Federal Building, where he was arraigned on charges of mail fraud before Commissioner Alexander J. Gilchrist.[39] At the arraignment, Flagg and the others were represented by Irving E. Ziegler, who had been counsel to Flagg for nine years. Assistant U.S. Attorney Abel F. Smith represented the government. All of the prisoners pleaded not guilty and asked for a hearing before Gilchrist, rather than have their cases sent to the Grand Jury.[40]

Gilchrist scheduled a hearing for the following Wednesday, September 27, and set bail at $25,000 for Flagg and lesser amounts for the others. When Zeigler complained that the bail was excessive, U.S. Attorney Henry A. Wise pointed out Flagg's criminal record, and the protest was ignored. Flagg said he then offered a cash bond, but was told that only a real estate bond would be acceptable. But by the time he could obtain such a bond, the commissioner had left town for his country home, and Flagg and seven of his friends were required to spend Saturday and Sunday nights in the Tombs.[41]

The Sunday newspapers were all over the story, drawn not only by Flagg's notoriety, but also by the prominence of Morgan and some of Flagg's other erstwhile luncheon companions.[42] Arrested along with Flagg and Morgan were Edward L. Schiller, who handled the money in Flagg's office, the Rev. James T. Schock, a Dutch Reformed minister, Joshua Brown, and Harry Jackson—all of whom brought business into the house. Flagg's counsel, Alvin M. Higgins, was arrested at his office, while Neely was taken at the restaurant. In addition, seven to ten women, purported to be "customers" of Flagg, including Keyes, were in the office when police entered, but they would not be charged.[43]

A *Tribune* article characterized Flagg's business in terms of "the old Miller Syndicate[44] and Storey cotton operations,[45] which wrecked thousands of investors." It went on to describe the process as creating a blind pool for investing money in stocks, with a portion of all money received from new investors set aside to pay dividends to older investors every Saturday. "As long as he could keep the money of new subscribers flowing into his treasury he could pay out 1 per cent a week to customers on his books and still have a splendid reserve on hand." Splendid indeed. Inspectors estimated that Flagg had taken in more than $1.5 million in the past two years, with customers in every large city in the country. The 1% per week payout "thoroughly captivated" his customers, so that few of them asked to withdraw their funds and many increased their accounts with Flagg.[46]

Flagg required his customers to sign contracts authorizing him to buy for the customer's "account and risk" ten shares of each of fifteen named stocks, all standard shares on the New York Stock Exchange, to be sold for the customer when the purchase showed a profit of one point or better and to be bought back whenever the price was a point or more "below the high." The reverse of this operation was to be employed with another list of nineteen stocks.

New York Stock Exchange ca. 1908

Flagg's commission charges under the contracts were to be one-fourth of 1 percent for buying and the same for selling. The contracts also authorized Flagg to loan all securities deposited with him or carried by him for customers and to pledge them as collateral for Flagg's loans.[47]

Flagg showed reporters a stack of blank contracts. "It is open and above board and refutes the charge that I guaranteed fabulous interest," he said. "I can pay every dollar I owe. I have handled $1,100,000 during the three years or more that I have been in business and I can account for every cent of it, every transaction. I have nothing to fear. This is all a vile conspiracy, cooked up by big brokers and Wall Street interests that are jealous of me."[48] Flagg would later ascribe the postal inspectors' assault on his operations to revenge for the $50,000 libel suit he filed against the New York *World* for having printed that he had been convicted of renting flats for immoral purposes.[49]

The prisoners spent a quiet Sunday in the Tombs, since no visitors were allowed. They occupied four cells on the seventh and top tier, known as the federal tier, because theirs was a federal case. Their breakfast and lunch were served by the Tombs caterer, though they were free to order from an outside restaurant. Up at 6 a.m., they took compulsory walks around their gallery, along with the fifty-plus other prisoners on the tier, three times during the day. Otherwise, the time was spent reading newspapers and writing press releases.[50]

Flagg's release, as quoted by various newspapers, began,

> They say I am running a "Miller Syndicate." If this is so, let them bring forward—let them show the one customer to whom I have ever paid a dollar out of his or any other customer's money, and I will make no further protest against their high-handed proceedings. Every dollar made in profits on closed transactions has been honorably made. When a customer has purchased stock, the date, the price and the name of the Stock Exchange broker from whom the stock was bought has been sent to the customer. When the customer sold his stock, the date, the price and the name of the Stock Exchange broker to whom the stock was sold was sent to the customer—with a check for the difference, less commission, tax and interest.
>
> These profits made on closed transactions have averaged more than 50 per cent a year for the first three and a half

years. Had no money been made on closed transactions, no money would have been paid out. After having conducted business on this basis for almost four years, I am arrested and accused of "intending" to defraud a person who has never had an account with me and to whom no "misrepresentations" have been made.

P.S. The arrest of my friends and employees, who have absolutely no voice in my business, is an outrage beyond words.

JARED FLAGG[51]

Morgan also expressed "outrage" at his arrest and arraignment. "It is the first time that I have been deprived of my liberty for a single minute," he told reporters. "So far as I know, Mr. Flagg is not guilty of a single dishonest act. Of the amount I have invested with him, I have not lost a single penny, but have received my dividends promptly, according to his policy."[52]

Most colorful was Higgins's statement:

The facts related in "Flagg's Flats," a book that crooks don't like to read, were employed by malicious men in connection with the grandstand play made Saturday when the threats of a clique here in New York to get even with Mr. Flagg were carried out. Russia has not persecuted the Jews more than a bunch of criminals have hounded him. I have been his friend and shall continue to be and to live in New York City.

FLAGG'S FLATS

BY
JARED FLAGG

Third Edition

Copyright, 1909, by Jessie Flagg

When the truth comes out in open court it will show that the officials have been imposed upon and lied to by cowards who do not dare come out in the open. If the legitimate buying and selling of real stock through real brokers and an accounting for every cent of profits and liability to customers is wrong, then the Stock Exchange couldn't do business one day.

Not a single customer of Mr. Flagg has ever complained and every one of them will stand by him. He has been square with them. This attack on him comes from outsiders whose solicitude for Mr. Flagg's satisfied customers is hypocritical. The many strong assurances of backing from my friends in New York to-day are splendid and most gratifying.[53]

It fell to U.S. Attorney Wise to respond to these statements: "I went over all the evidence in this case before I would consent to the issuance of warrants. We have a perfect case. In all the similar prosecutions we have undertaken we have transferred the headquarters of the get-rich-quick gentlemen from New York to the Federal Prison in Atlanta, Ga. Flagg has been giving out statements in his own handwriting since his arrest. These statements are evidence in themselves that he had foreseen arrest and devised a defense, for each of them is practically a repetition of the other."[54]

On Sunday afternoon, Zeigler told the press that Ernest and Montague Flagg would put up the total $67,500 bail set for all the prisoners.[55] On Monday, Flagg's brother, the architect Ernest Flagg, put up two of his properties at 109 and 111 East 40th Street, valued at $250,000, but subject to a mortgage of $100,000.[56] Ernest took care of the bond for his brother and Edward Schiller; other prisoners found sureties to guarantee their appearances.[57]

Madeline Russe

Warrants were issued for nineteen-year-old Madeline Russe, who was alleged to be Flagg's private secretary,[58] and for Elbridge C. Sewall, a cashier in Flagg's office. Authorities were also looking for Flagg's agent, William B. Reed. Sewell was arrested that evening while leaving for his summer home in Quogue, Long Island.[59] Russe reportedly went into hiding, first declining, then agreeing, to testify before a grand jury that had already begun looking into the Flagg case. Her sister Belle was also said to be sought for questioning.[60]

Some of Flagg's customers rallied to his defense. Thomas E. Morford of the American Steam Pump Co., for example, told authorities the arrest of

Flagg was "a high-handed outrage. I am a customer of Mr. Flagg and am convinced of his honesty," Morford asserted at the arraignment. "On my investment of $1,000, which I made last April, I have been getting dividends regularly. The customers of Mr. Flagg will rally to his support." Other customers were not so sanguine and were reportedly seeking to have Flagg declared an involuntary bankrupt in order to gain control of some $400,000 he allegedly stored in safe deposit vaults.[61]

Once free from jail, Flagg invited anyone who cared to hear his side of the story to join him at Café des Beaux Arts.[62] There, Flagg declared, "I have known of this investigation of my affairs for two months, and I know what I am talking about when I say it was prompted by my refusal to transfer my business from one chain of brokers to another." Flagg said he would bring a conspiracy suit against eight men, and that he had copies of seven affidavits showing that improper influence was brought against Miss Russe. "The moment these become public," Flagg is said to have shouted, "a prominent member of the Consolidated Exchange will resign." Flagg also said he would give $100,000 to charity if anyone could prove his transactions were not honest.[63]

Not to be outdone by Flagg's public relations campaign, Postmaster General Frank H. Hitchcock called this case "one of the most important that the Post Office Department has handled for years. I want to

U.S. District Judge E. Henry Lacombe

express my gratification to the inspectors here on the manner in which they have handled it." Inspector Kincaid also got ex-U.S. Treasurer Morgan to modify his position somewhat. While Morgan expressed continued confidence in Flagg, he said he was "willing to shift my point of view if it can be shown that Flagg's business was as crooked as you say it is."[64]

Meanwhile, Flagg had obtained an order from U.S. District Judge Emile Henry Lacombe requiring U.S. Attorney Wise and Marshal Henkel to show cause why records of his business seized in Saturday's raid should not be returned.[65] Flagg's lawyer, Robert C. Beatty, presented an affidavit concluding that Wise and Henkel had no authority to make any seizure of books and papers, and that their removal hampered not only Flagg's business but also the preparation of his defense. Wise and Henkel responded that Flagg's books had never been in their possession, but rather were seized by police and were now being held by the Post Office Department in support of their complaint before Commissioner Gilchrist. Judge Lacombe ruled on September 26 that, under the circumstances, he could not order Wise to give up something he never had, and suggested that Flagg's only recourse was a civil lawsuit to recover goods wrongly taken. The grand jury was expected to hand up indictments as early as Wednesday morning.[66]

Endnote

Also on September 26, Flagg's brother Ernest submitted a moving defense of Jared to the press. The *New York Times* printed the letter in its entirety:

> I and other members of the family to which he belongs are proud to claim relationship with Jared Flagg. We are not ignorant of his faults, the worst of which is an apparently uncontrollable habit of exaggeration, nor are we unacquainted with his perfect honesty and other good qualities, which far outweigh them. If we did not know him to be utterly incapable of what has been ascribed to him we should be overwhelmed with shame.

> Jared Flagg comes of stock which does not produce criminals. Since 1637 on the paternal side, and since 1650 on the maternal side our people have borne honorable records in this country, and many estimable and useful citizens have been numbered among them, but none more able and, in many respects, remarkable than he of whom I speak; and I may also say there has never been one so misunderstood and misrepresented by those who do not know him personally, as this same Jared Flagg.

> I shall not attempt to defend him for he is perfectly able to defend himself if his books and papers are restored to him; but I want to protest against what seems to be one of the most

high-handed and outrageous persecutions to which innocent people were ever subjected.

With no other excuse than that someone suspected he might do something wrong in the future, his office was raided, his books and papers seized, he, his friends, customers, and clerks dragged off to jail by people acting in the name of the United States. While the newspapers, without a scrap of evidence, and in spite of statements of esteem and confidence from those who were interested personally in his financial operations, and who knew most about what he was doing, treat him as a common swindler, put words in his mouth which could only be uttered by a low braggart, call his assistants "cappers," whatever that may mean, and hold perfectly innocent and honorable gentlemen up to scorn and insult, simply because they happen to be in his company.

The whole proceeding is shameful, but not for them or him.

My brother, his family, and friends are able to regard what has been done with composure, because they know that it is only a question of time when this shame will be placed where it justly belongs.

ERNEST FLAGG

New York, Sept. 26, 1911

Chapter 5

Flagg's Trial

The federal grand jury indicted Flagg and his eight associates for mail fraud on Wednesday, September 27, 1911. Flagg, Morgan, Schiller, Schock, Jackson, Brown, Sewall, and Higgins, all of whom were already out on bail, and Neeley, who remained in the Tombs, had appeared in court in anticipation of an examination before Commissioner Gilchrist. Instead, members of the grand jury filed into the courtroom, and Gilchrist withdrew in favor of U.S. District Court Judge Charles M. Hough, who took his seat on the bench to receive the indictment. After a brief pause to have an error in the indictment corrected, Hough summoned the defendants to enter a plea. All pleaded not guilty and their bail was continued.

The indictment specifically named Bertha L. Bentley of Corry, Pa., and Julia E. Wood of Reading, Pa., as intended victims of Flagg's fraudulent scheme, alleging that the "false, fraudulent, and fictitious" representations made by Flagg and associates were made to convert the money obtained by these women and other investors to the defendant's own use.[1]

Reporters covering the Flagg story seemed distracted by a tale of mysterious women, perhaps hoping to find a juicy sex scandal to brighten their stories on investments and indictments. At the center of the tale was Madeline Russe, the nineteen-year-old beauty whose relationship to Flagg was variously described as telephone operator, confidential secretary, and even fiancée. The *Times* described Russe's role in this story as "a little indefinite," pointing out that she was named in the original complaint, but not indicted. At one point, Flagg accused her of revealing his secrets to a "downtown broker" in a "fit of pique."[2] The elusive Miss Russe finally surfaced on Friday, September 29, at the Federal Building, where she met with Assistant District Attorney Claude A. Thompson for two to three hours. She had received assurances from Flagg's lawyer, John F. McIntyre, that bail would be provided if she were arrested and that McIntyre would represent her. She was not arrested, Thompson told reporters, and would be available to testify if needed.[3]

Hazel Murray

According to one account, Russe agreed to testify against Flagg because she was jealous of Flagg's attention to another woman in Flagg's office, one Hazel Murray,[4] who was said to be one of Flagg's protégés from his theatrical agent days. Flagg "was just lovely," Murray is purported to have said, "and promised to make a great actress of me."[5] Yet another woman made an appearance in the press accounts. "A mysteriously veiled young woman," who testified before the grand jury, was identified only as "an employee of a New York newspaper, who had furnished the government with important evidence."[6] Flagg would later identify her as a *World* reporter named Rand.[7]

There were other diversions from the legal proceedings as well. Flagg himself alleged that some $12,000 in securities had disappeared from his office following the raid.[8] Those securities were later found in Flagg's safe.[9] Some newspapers focused on Flagg investors, such as Buffalo Alderman Elmer E. Harris, who took a flyer on Flagg's operation and reaped 1% per week in dividends before it all came crashing down. "I'm not out more than would buy a suit of clothes," he said, "so there isn't much use talking about it."[10] Another investor, Edward C. DeWolfe of Chicago, was said to have invested $220,000, based on an examination of Flagg's books. DeWolfe denied he had invested that much, though he conceded that he was a "heavy" investor and acted as a "kind of agent" for Flagg in Chicago. He said he, too, was receiving a 1% per week return and was "absolutely sure that everything will come out all right."[11] Flagg said DeWolfe was sending letters from Flagg's office to reassure investors that "everything was all right."[12] Indeed, a group of forty-five investors signed a letter expressing confidence in Flagg:

> We are some of the customers of Jared Flagg, having intrusted (sic) to him our own money in various sums running into thousands of dollars. We have absolute confidence in the integrity and ability of Mr. Flagg. He has always kept his word.
>
> Now, we wish to know why a few malicious outsiders insist upon Mr. Flagg turning our money over to hostile strangers, who only want to break up the business which we have intrusted (sic) to Mr. Flagg.
>
> Newspaper reports have gone out that are so outrageously false and one-sided as to be grotesque. They would be humorous except for the fact that they might influence customers miles removed from here who have no opportunity to secure real information.
>
> The interruption of the business of Mr. Flagg may involve a temporary suspension of profit to his customers.
>
> It was, and is, the intention of those who engineered the outrage to wreck the business built up by Mr. Flagg. The only way these outsiders could possibly succeed would be through the weak-heartedness of his customers.
>
> We, who are among them, who know of the injustice of the proceedings, are issuing this, knowing that representatives of those who seek the undoing of Mr. Flagg have been working furiously to get customers to sign a petition to bring about bankruptcy.
>
> Bankruptcy proceedings are what the outsiders seek. We ask all of Flagg's customers to stand as one against such methods.[13]

Notwithstanding the indictment that was handed up on September 27, the grand jury continued to take testimony through the fall. Madeline Russe and her sister, Belle, were among those giving new evidence, along with DeWolfe and others. It became apparent that prosecutors contemplated seeking a new indictment, based on a closer examination of Flagg's books, before putting Flagg and the other defendants on trial.

Flagg sought to head off any such action by filing a motion on September 26 to compel the District Attorney and the U.S Marshal to return to him "certain books, papers, articles of personal property, and cash" that had been forcibly taken from his 40th Street offices. In his opinion denying that motion, Judge Lacombe said it appeared that neither the Marshal nor the District Attorney, nor any of their deputies or assistants, took the books, papers, and property described, nor had the books in their possession, but rather that the materials were in the hands of the Post Office authorities.[14]

As for Flagg's business, a "protective committee" of Flagg's customers was formed in late October to wind up the stock fund. The committee sent Flagg's investors a form asking them to sign over authority to close out their accounts. "The committee of the customers of Jared Flagg desire to close out as the opportunity may occur the open commitments on your account," the committee wrote, "with a view of not only paying to you your original margin in full but such additional profits as may be made while closing your commitments and without any loss to you."[15]

Flagg endorsed the committee's work. "To My Customers: I asked you to stand by me and you certainly did stand. You stood by to a man. Not one showed the white feather,[16] and to say that I am astounded—to say that I am gratified—does not express how I feel. Now, I have another

The
Flagg
Raid

25 Cents

favor to ask. Stand by the Customers' Committee. These men are working like Trojans and in full accord with your interests. Authorize them to act in your behalf. JARED FLAGG."[17]

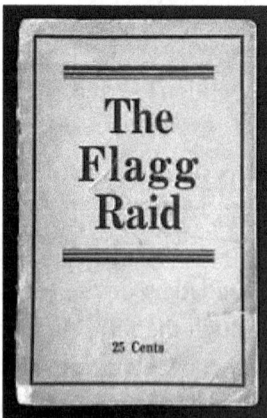

Throughout the fall and winter of 1911–12, Flagg worked on his book "The Flagg Raid," recounting the events that brought him to this precarious point up to January 23, 1912. Flagg would claim to have had 62,000 copies of "Raid" printed by the

Charles Francis Press and a copy sent to every lawyer in Greater New York and Washington, D.C. "Also to every postmaster, congressman, senator, and high office holder in the United States," he wrote. "Many copies were sold in news-stands, especially at the Park Row Building, in which the offices of Claude A. Thompson were located; and if it was the ambition of this young man's life to convict me before the point of my pen had pricked him can you imagine his aspirations after it had commenced to puncture him?" Flagg quoted Thompson as declaring that "within thirty days I shall have Flagg eating on tin plates in Atlanta [federal penitentiary]."[18]

Flagg also met frequently over lunch with his brother Ernest and his lawyer, Robert C. Beatty, whom Ernest had recommended, to discuss the book and his case.[19] The newspapers, however, found little to write about the case beyond a *contretemps* in the offices of Mr. Thompson, who allegedly "shoved" Belle Russe out of his office, prompting her to sue him for $1,000.[20] The anticipated superseding indictment was not handed up until July 17, 1912.

The new indictment named Flagg, Morgan, Sewall, Higgins, Jackson, and Schock, and three new defendants, DeWolfe and James Allen, Flagg's agents in Chicago, and Rufus P. Hankey, Flagg's agent in Detroit. Brown, Neely, and Schiller were not reindicted. The new indictment consisted of seven counts and was 55 pages long in printed form.[21] Count 1 captures the essence of the indictment, charging that Flagg and his co-defendants:

THE CONSOLIDATED STOCK EXCHANGE

Consolidated Stock Exchange

unlawfully and knowingly devised a scheme and artifice to
defraud and for obtaining money and property by means of
false and fraudulent pretenses, representations, promises and
devices from divers persons whose names are to the Jurors
unknown hereinafter referred to as the persons so intended
to be defrauded....

The first count goes on to describe the scheme in great detail.
Specifically, the indictment said investors' money would be aggregated or
divided into "units" of $10,000; these units would be divided into two
"classes." On behalf of the investors in the first of those classes, Flagg
would purchase corporate stocks, in ten-share "lots," through brokers on
the New York and Consolidated Stock Exchanges. For the same investors,
Flagg would also sell short other corporate stocks. For the second class of
investors, Flagg would sell short the very stocks purchased for the first
class and purchase the very stocks he had sold short for the first class.

Flagg then falsely told investors that, for each unit, he would
purchase additional ten-share lots of stock at the market price, plus an
additional ten-share lot of each stock that declined one point or more.
These shares would be held by Flagg or his brokers until their prices rose
one point or more, at which point those shares would be sold. Flagg would
also contract to sell short any shares that rose one point or more; those
contracts would be held open until the stock dropped one point or more.
Then, Flagg would cover and close the short sales, realizing a profit of one
point or more on each share sold.

Brokers would be under strict instructions never to sell any shares
or close out any short sales, except at a price that would show a profit on
each completed transaction. Thus, Flagg represented that he had been
earning upwards of fifty percent a year without sustaining any actual
losses, since no shares were ever sold at a loss.

The indictment's first count also alleged that Flagg and his co-
defendants falsely and fraudulently represented that all transactions would
be carried out through licensed brokers and that Flagg would report all
purchases and sales to investors. Proceeds from the scheme would be paid
out to investors on a weekly basis, in amounts upwards of 50% annually.

Flagg represented that he would charge investors only one quarter
of one percent on the par value of each share purchased or sold, plus six

percent annual interest on any money Flagg would lend to investors for the purpose of carrying the shares purchased or sold short on their behalf. There would be no further charge for Flagg's services, and Flagg would receive no further compensation for acting as agent for his investors. In fact, the indictment charged, Flagg received a secret rebate on the commissions charged by Flagg's brokers, while reporting to investors the full amount of commissions paid. He also received additional funds from investors which he falsely claimed were reimbursements for money paid by him as dividends on account of short sales reportedly made and kept open on their behalf. He also converted some of the investors' money to his own use, disguised as salary, drawing accounts, commissions, compensation for services, or profits.

Flagg allegedly maintained an "elaborate, fraudulent and deceptive set of books" in which the purchases and sales of shares that Flagg actually made through brokers would be entered in such a manner as to mislead investors into thinking that the scheme was extremely profitable. In fact, Flagg was not buying, selling, and holding shares according to his system, but rather "from day to day making sales substantially equal in number to the purchases, and often at approximately the same or lower prices," so that he was in fact holding, or carrying with brokers, few if any of the large number of shares or short sale contracts that he would represent to his investors.

Count 1 concluded with the allegation that Flagg used the mail to carry out his illicit scheme. As evidence, count 1 charged that he sent a four-page circular outlining his scheme to a Mr. F. H. Iden of New Brighton, Pa.[22] This mailing was reiterated in counts 4[23] and 7.[24] Other counts offered additional uses of the mails to defraud, including a notice of purchase and sale of shares sent to Mr. S. Campbell of New York City (counts 2[25] and 3[26]), and two contracts and two receipts sent to the Rev. J.C. France of Bridgeport, Conn. (counts 5,[27] 6[28] and 7[29]).

Count 7 was framed as a conspiracy charge and so reiterated the explanation of the scheme first described in counts 1 and 6. Count 7 also included a letter sent by co-defendant, James Allen, Flagg's Chicago agent, to Flagg himself, listing the prospective investors whom he planned to contact in the coming days and weeks. It also included a letter from co-defendant James Schock, who worked out of Flagg's 40th St. office, to one J.D. Verplanck. The Schock letter is characteristic of the Flagg sales pitch:

> We began just about three years ago without a single customer. Today we have somewhat more than 575 customers for whom we have made thus far over $300,000; and so rapid and great is our present growth that we shall in this one year alone pay them more than $350,000 in actual, genuine profits.
>
> Every customer's profits have averaged about 50 per cent. per annum—paid at the rate of about one per cent. per week.
>
> All early customers (probably about 200) have received back in profits all or more than all they put in, and yet their accounts continue as profitable as ever. My first investment has paid me 186% thus far.
>
> Behind *every* customer's money there is now much more than half a million dollars mutually pledged for its security and safety; and this backing is increasing at the rate of about $60,000 per month now, and soon the rate will be $100,000 at least. Everyone's security is growing greater by the week.
>
> Such an opportunity to make money without any danger of losing is exceedingly rare.

**U.S. District Judge
Learned Hand**

> The privilege of getting into such a "club" as ours is something to prize.
>
> This matter will fully repay your most careful and scrutinizing consideration.[30]

Flagg and several of the other defendants appeared before Judge Learned Hand on Thursday, July 18, and pleaded not guilty to the charges. Hand continued the bail under which the defendants had been released on the previous indictment. The

**U.S. District
Judge Charles M. Hough**

other defendants were to appear later,[31] but one of them, the Rev. Schock, died within the month of "intestinal troubles."[32]

There were no further developments in the Flagg case until December 2, 1912, when one of Flagg's attorneys, Wade H. Ellis, filed a demurrer to the charges against him.[33] Arguments were heard by Judge Charles M. Hough, who overruled the demurrer in early February. "The substantive charges came down to this," Hough said, "that Flagg pretended to speculate in stocks for the benefit of customers; he did not do it, yet paid them money as if he had speculated profitably, and then sought to obtain additional customers by representing how profitable had been the operations of first comers. Nothing but a trial can show whether this story is true."[34]

With the demurrers to their indictments having been overruled, Flagg and company again pleaded not guilty in U.S. District Court on February 16. Trial was set for the March term and bail bonds were continued in all cases.[35] In fact, the trial did not begin until October 19, 1914, and Flagg largely kept his name out of the newspapers until then.[36] According to Flagg, however, Assistant U.S. District Attorney Thompson was extremely busy during the delay.

> Thirty days passed—a thousand days passed—during which time Prosecutor Thompson poured out the people's money. He engaged several accountants and after they had worked three years on my stolen books making, under his direction, straight entries appear crooked, and after discrediting my most important witnesses by having them indicted, and after devising and revising one hundred and forty-two lies, as itemized in my "bill of exceptions" he finally felt prepared to trick a jury into rendering a verdict against me.[37]

When court finally convened on October 19, Flagg and Beatty tried once again to have the indictment quashed, this time arguing that two of the grand jurors, including the foreman Adam C. Arneff and Michael Kehoe, were notorious, professional jurymen and Kehoe a self-confessed gambler. Beatty argued that one conviction had already been overturned because of Kehoe's presence on the grand jury, but Thompson responded that the conviction was overturned because Kehoe had served on a closely related grand jury, not because he was a professional juryman or gambler.[38]

The motion was denied by presiding Judge Frank H. Rudkin,[39] who also ruled that Flagg's codefendants would be tried separately and that Flagg could represent himself at trial, provided Beatty assisted as attorney of record. Asked by reporters why he chose to represent himself, Flagg acknowledged that he was not a lawyer, but asserted that he knew more about his case than anyone else. "I am an honest man prevented from making an honest living and I want the world to know about it," he declared.[40]

Jury selection began that afternoon with the selection of twelve prospective jurors, seven of whom were peremptorily challenged by Flagg the following day.[41] After twenty-three additional prospective jurors were questioned, a jury was finally empaneled and sworn on Tuesday afternoon, October 20, 1914, and the trial was underway, now with a new attorney, John M. Coleman, representing Flagg. But before the government could present an opening statement, Coleman alerted the court to his desire to renew Flagg's 1911 motion for return of his books and papers—which he did as soon as the government's opening statement was concluded.

In his opening statement, Thompson told the jury that Flagg had failed to live up to his written and oral agreements with his investors. After obtaining control of their money, he said, Flagg "ceased to carry the stocks on the market and resorted to the subterfuge of selling and buying the same amount of stocks a day, so that there was no broker's commission to pay, but which fact did not prevent him from charging his commission. This ruse enabled him to collect on an average $600,000 a year, or the amount that should have gone to brokers if the sales had been bona fide ones."

Thompson said Flagg had lost more than $150,000 in stock speculation over the past four years.[42]

When Thompson concluded, Coleman renewed his motion for return of Flagg's books and papers. Since those books and papers were now under the control of the U.S. District Attorney—rather than the Post Office, as they had been in 1911—Coleman asked Judge Rudkin to order them returned. "[Y]ou cannot make a man testify against himself," Coleman argued, "the Constitution guarantees every man against search and seizure."[43]

**U.S. District
Judge Frank M. Rudkin**

A.D.A. Thompson argued that Flagg and his previous counsel had been advised that they might have access to any of the books and papers at any time in order to prepare their defense. They had taken advantage of that, he said, by having accountants there examining those books and papers. Thompson's superior, U.S. District Attorney H. Snowden Marshall, added that Flagg made no attempt to recover his papers from the postal authorities, as had been suggested by Judge Lacombe, and that the prosecution had no warning that Flagg would renew his motion at trial.[44]

Judge Rudkin then asked the prosecutors whether the police or postal inspectors had warrants authorizing them to seize anything when Flagg was arrested. All of the lawyers had referred to the recently decided case of *United States v. Weeks*, in which the U.S. Supreme Court held that the seizure of a defendant's personal papers without a warrant, even if incident to arrest, constituted a violation of the defendant's Fourth and Fifth Amendment rights and that admitting those papers at trial constituted reversible error.[45] Marshall told Rudkin there had been no warrant except for Flagg's arrest, but argued that Flagg had "substantially acquiesce[d]" in possession of the papers by the District Attorney by delaying any action to recover them for some two years.[46]

In fact, shortly before the trial began, Flagg's former lawyers, Robert Beatty and Wade Ellis, had petitioned the U.S. Supreme Court for a writ of mandamus to force the government to return the papers and a writ of prohibition to halt the trial.[47] Judge Rudkin said he thought the High Court would decide the matter before the trial was concluded. "My own private opinion is that the constitutional rights of this defendant were invaded without any warrant or authority of law whatever," he said, "but I will deny the motion at this time and correct myself later if I conclude I am in error, and if the Supreme Court of the United States does not pass upon it before I reach it."[48] The newspapers reported that Flagg smiled for the first time since the trial began.[49]

In view of Rudkin's unexpected expression of personal opinion, Marshall and his team took a five-minute recess, then offered to withdraw the government's opposition to Flagg's motion and turn over the books and papers to Flagg. "We do not want to start the case with any course of conduct on the part of the Government that does not seem fair to your Honor and does not seem correct in every way," Marshall said. Coleman agreed to take charge of the materials, reportedly telling Rudkin that Flagg now had the right to "engulf them in the waters of New York Bay."[50] Presumably, that never happened. Thompson proceeded to examine his first witness, then the court adjourned until the following day so the books could be transferred to Flagg's offices.[51]

During the discussion about returning Flagg's papers, nothing was said by either party or the judge about admitting them into evidence and taking testimony derived from their analysis. But the first-time prosecutors attempted to elicit such testimony, from Flagg's margin clerk, Mrs. A.B. Childs, Coleman objected on the ground that any evidence she gave would be derived from the papers that had been illegally seized. Judge Rudkin overruled the objection and Coleman took an exception, a pattern that would continue throughout the trial with every government witness.[52]

Over the next few days, Flagg seemed to gain the upper hand. Pointing his pince-nez at government witnesses, whom he cross-examined himself, Flagg elicited expressions of satisfaction with the dividends they received by investing with Flagg. And when Thompson read excerpts from Flagg's book, "How to Take Money Out of Wall Street," the reaction in the courtroom suggested that the jurors were more amused than offended by Flagg. Among the entries from an appendix titled "Flagg's Philosophies and Wall Street Dictionary":

> "Account"—A monthly reminder of what an ass you have made of yourself.

> "Bear"—A two-legged animal who is never happy unless others are miserable.

> "Bull"—A simple-minded, hopeful creature who looks on the bright side of things, but is rarely happy.

> "Bucket Shop"—A place where you can bet $5 or $5,000 on any stock. You are permitted to do the guessing, but the proprietor takes the money.

> "Curb Stone Broker"—A man with big ideas and small aspirations.

> "Flyer"—An occasional desire to be reckless.

> "Interest"—That which makes brokers rich and customers poor.

> "Lamb"—A well-read man who, like the sucker at poker, is inquisitive and pays the penalty.

> "Panic"—A settled state of affairs.

> "Pointer"—An expert liar.

> "Professional Gambler"—One who bets on a certainty.

> "Pool"—A syndicate of men who combine to dupe the public and, failing this, dupe each other.

At one point, the courtroom became so loud with laughter that Rudkin ordered Thompson to stop reading.[53]

But on October 26, Flagg's luck seemed to change. The U.S. Supreme Court denied Flagg's petition,[54] without opinion, and Thomson produced his star witness: Henry D. Mildeberger, Flagg's former lawyer and head bookkeeper.[55] Mildeberger first met Flagg when he served as Flagg's attorney in libel suits he initiated against the *World* and other newspapers.[56] In early 1908, Mildeberger drew up partnership papers for The Jared Flagg Company. He became regularly employed by the company in the summer of 1908, when he devised a bookkeeping system for the business based on transaction slips and brokers' notices he received from the "front room." Mildeberger said he had nothing to do with ordering stocks from brokers nor with assigning any particular transaction to a particular unit or customer.[57]

When Thompson attempted to introduce a document based on that system, however, Coleman objected to any testimony based on the books and papers taken in the raid. Rudkin overruled the objection, unconvinced by Coleman's analogy to a confession elicited by extortion. "I may be in error, but if I am some higher court will have to correct me," he said, inviting Coleman to file an exception.[58]

Mildeberger proceeded to testify in great detail as to how he kept the books, comparing transaction slips and brokers' notices for consistency, if not accuracy, and how he allocated profits assigned by the front room to a particular unit among the investors who held an interest in that unit. Because each unit represented an aggregate investment of $10,000, and Flagg accepted investments as low as $25, Mildeberger divided the profits into fortieths and allocated them according to how many fortieths each investor owned. Asked if he ever knew whether the profit shown on the transaction slips had actually been made, Mildeberger said he did not,[59] but later testified that he never received a transaction slip reporting closed transactions that did not show a profit.[60]

Mildeberger also described the procedures by which weekly checks were distributed to customers based on the profits they had earned that week. Again, however, Mildeberger said that the "amounts of checks were based entirely upon information that came to me from the front room, but I don't know whether the money had been made or not which was being paid out as profits."[61] Mildeberger also described the payment of commissions and compensation to Flagg's various agents, some of whom were customers, while others were not. In all, he said, there were about 114 men in that category.[62]

In the afternoon, Mildeberger testified that, in all, Flagg had received $1,155,560 from his customers and returned $522,522 to them in profits.[63] Flagg conducted the cross examination himself, eliciting Mildeberger's belief that the business was honest. "During the year that you were in my employ," Flagg asked, "did I ever—did I or anyone ever suggest to you to make any entry that would be irregular in any way?" Mildeberger answered, "There never was a suggestion."[64]

The government's final witnesses, testifying on October 28, were Grover C. Trumbull and J.P. Fensler, accountants for the Department of Justice, who testified that the books of the brokers with whom Flagg dealt showed a loss of $138,249, compared to profits of only $1,934, while Flagg's books recorded profits from the same transactions of $687,965 and no losses.[65] When the government rested shortly thereafter,[66] Coleman then made a series of motions to strike all testimony based on Flagg's books and records and, ultimately, to dismiss the case altogether. Rudkin denied all of the defense motions, and adjourned until October 29.[67]

Jared Flagg, Jr.

When court resumed, Flagg gave the opening statement for the defense, a long, rambling, exculpatory lecture about his system that drew repeated objections from the government and repeated admonitions from the judge.[68] At one point, Rudkin offered to "simplify matters" by announcing that he would instruct the jurors that Flagg's system was "not fraudulent in itself, and that the only question on this trial is as to whether or not it had been followed out."[69]

Coleman jumped on that statement. "We have never had that open concession," he exclaimed. "You have never conceded that on the record, have you?" Thompson interjected that he had said as much in his opening statement, and the judge instructed the jury to eliminate the legality of Flagg's system from further consideration. So, Flagg asked, "[i]f followed the method would work, is that the idea?" Rudkin replied, "Whether or not it would work is not material. It was not fraudulent, the people just simply took their chance."[70] For more than an hour, Flagg continued to argue his case, even encouraging and fielding questions from the jury, to the point that Thompson requested the privilege of cross examining him.[71] When he finally finished, he politely thanked the jury for its attention.[72]

The defense began calling its witnesses, including several investors who testified on October 30 that they were fully satisfied with their investments and understood the risks involved. Flagg's treasurer, Elbert C. Sewell, testified that Flagg had paid out more than $600,000 in profits to his customers.[73] Flagg even recalled Henry Mildeberger to testify that he was compensated by the government for his analysis of Flagg's books.[74] Flagg's last witness was Daniel N. Morgan, the former U.S. Treasurer and alleged co-conspirator. Morgan described his stake in Flagg's business, the minimal amount of work he did for Flagg, and his compensation of one-half percent of the business done each year, plus commissions on any new business he brought in. He also affirmed that he had never lost confidence in Flagg, and he avoided every effort by Thompson on cross examination to shake that confidence. "I believed and still believe that Mr. Flagg's business was honest and straightforward," he declared.[75]

After resting his case, Coleman again moved to strike all testimony based on Flagg's papers and to dismiss the case for lack of evidence. Rudkin denied the motions and adjourned until Monday, November 2.[76] When court resumed, Thompson summed up for the government:

> Gentlemen, I have here a statement prepared, under my
> direction, by Government Accountants. It shows the true

condition of Flagg's affairs September 23, 1911, and I want you to take it with you to the jury room, I want you to examine it, ponder over it, and bring in a verdict in accordance with the facts it reveals....[77]

[R]ead these contracts—I got them all together—and see what was represented in the literature. Take the brokers' statements and see if you can find the profits made in Wall Street. See if you can find the profits that came from Wall Street. Take the analyses which show that not one dollar of that money that was paid out in the guise of profits came from Wall Street. Take those exhibits and every one of them, if you wish, to the jury room and examine them, and if you do so I am sure that you will find that they bear out what I have stated to you.[78]

Coleman declared the government's whole case was a frame-up, pointing out that the government had not been able to produce a single client to file a complaint, nor show that any one of them had ever closed out his account. Coleman asked the jury to understand that there were certain interests in Wall Street that desired to see Flagg closed up.[79] Flagg would write later that his lawyer objected strenuously to Thompson's closing on the ground that the government-prepared statement was "absolutely false."

[I]t represented the broker, Mr. Flagg, to be the speculator; that it charged up to him shrinkages in his customers' accounts—amounting to over five hundred thousand dollars—whereas, his customers were responsible to him for those shrinkages; that they had put up as margin over one million dollars in cash for the express purpose of protecting him against such shrinkages; that in law, and in equity, and in all justice, Mr. Flagg was only responsible to his customers for their credit balances. Mr. Flagg was not running a bucket shop or conducting a discretionary pool. He was simply executing signed, specific, orders, just as any other stock broker would execute specific orders.[80]

Rudkin overruled Coleman's objection and proceeded to charge the jury.

I charge you as a matter of law that the plan or system described in the pamphlet, circulars and contracts received in evidence, is not a scheme or artifice to defraud or for obtaining money or property by means of false or fraudulent pretenses, representations, or promises, if honestly and fairly conducted. But it is for you to say, under the instructions of the Court, whether or not such plan or system constituted a scheme or artifice to defraud or for obtaining money or property by means of false and fraudulent pretenses, representations or promises as charged in the indictment, by reason of the manner in which the business was conducted by the defendant, or by reason of false and fraudulent pretenses, representations or promises made by the defendant concerning that plan or system....[81]

Rudkin suggested the jurors first consider the conspiracy charge in the seventh count of the indictment. "[I]f you find that that charge is established beyond a reasonable doubt, then the acts and declarations made by the several defendants in furtherance of the object of the conspiracy so formed are, in contemplation of the law, the acts of all the parties so conspiring, and binding on all." Otherwise, if the conspiracy charge were not proved, he said, the jury would have to reject all testimony relating to the actions of the alleged co-conspirators, unless Flagg "aided, abetted, counseled, commanded, induced or procured" the conduct of the others.[82]

What effect that suggestion may have had on the jury will never be known. The jury retired at 5:30 p.m. for dinner and deliberations, and returned with a verdict at 10:17 p.m. that night.[83] Oddly enough, considering the judge's recommendation, the jury acquitted Flagg on the conspiracy count, but found him guilty on all six other charges.[84] Barring a successful appeal, Flagg faced up to two years in prison, a $10,000 fine, or both.[85]

The New York *Evening World*, for one, was gleeful about the conviction. Lumping Flagg in with two other recently convicted swindlers, the paper called it "[a]ltogether a gratifying round-up."[86] Flagg recounted that flowers were placed on Thompson's desk and he was promoted to first assistant U.S. Attorney for the Southern District of New York, with a salary increase to $100 per week.[87]

Caught At Last! A Wolf Who Has Preyed On Innocent Girls for 25 Years

The Surprising Career of Jared Flagg, Jr., Who, After Long Outwitting the Police with His Ingenious Schemes, Is Entrapped by the United States Authorities

Jared Flagg's Various Schemes

Accounts differed as to Flagg's immediate reaction to the verdict. One newspaper report said he was "crushed," having been confident throughout the trial that the government would never be able to prove its case.[88] Another paper, however, said Flagg was "entirely unmoved," but merely leaned over to whisper something to his brother Ernest sitting behind him and to one side. Madeline Russe, who sat directly behind Flagg, "appeared to be more downcast over the verdict than her employer."[89] Much later, reflecting on the verdict, Flagg's attitude could best be characterized as indignant.

> Not one of those twelve men, on my jury, understood the [government's] statement to be, or realized that it was, a deliberate fraud, perpetrated by agents of the United States Government, banded together in a conspiracy to deceive them. They knew it simply as a Government Exhibit and thought it honest. And after examining it, and pondering over it four hours, they very naturally brought in a verdict in accordance with the lies which it did not reveal to them.[90]

The jury realized too late, Flagg wrote, that they had been "flabbergasted into pronouncing me guilty. To a man, they wanted to see their verdict reversed by the higher Court."[91]

Chapter 6

Victorious Appeal

Judge Rudkin heard arguments in support of Flagg's motion for a new trial on Friday, November 6, 1914. Flagg's attorney, John M. Coleman, again challenged the government's seizure of Flagg's books and papers and demanded a new trial on the ground that the raid violated Flagg's Fifth Amendment right against self-incrimination. Coleman also said the court had erred in allowing testimony and other evidence based on the wrongly seized books, by admitting promotional materials and statements prepared by Flagg's alleged co-conspirators, and by denying Flagg's various motions to dismiss.[1] When Coleman finished with the legal argument, Flagg jumped to his feet. Reporters described him as "carefully dressed, as he had been through all the trial, but his thin, pale face looked more drawn and sharply defined than it had been...."[2]

"I want a new trial," Flagg said, "because I did not have a fair trial. I cast no reflections upon your honor, but 999 men out of 1,000 do not understand the difference between an indictment and a verdict, and from the first moment I was considered a guilty man.

> I have no complaint to make of the trial itself. It was as fair as any I have heard of, but I have this to complain of: For a time I could swap blows with the prosecution without hindrance, but at the end, with my hands tied down, without power to defend myself, I was forced to receive blows not on my body or my face but beneath my belt.

Throughout his oration, which went on for half an hour, Flagg was prompted by his confidential secretary, Madeline Russe. He detailed the charges that Assistant District Attorney Claude A. Thompson had made in his closing statement to the jury, asserting that there was no evidence to support them. And he insisted that his business methods were no different from those of other brokers. "Why should I be selected from all the others? I must and do object that I should be made the goat." When Flagg finished, Thompson announced he had nothing to say, and Judge Rudkin said Flagg would remain free on his original $25,000 bail until his decision was announced on November 10.[3]

At Coleman's request, allegedly based on the discovery of new evidence,[4] Rudkin postponed his judgment for a week, but on November 17, he rejected Coleman's arguments on the law, particularly as to secondary evidence, stating that "the defendant must at his peril keep his documents from other eyes; if he does not he must suffer the consequences." Ruling further that the evidence warranted submitting the case to the jury, Rudkin repeated the refrain he had used at trial. "If I am in error in this, some other court will correct my error. The motion for a new trial is denied...."[5]

Flagg and Coleman made one last attempt to persuade Rudkin to grant Flagg a new trial, offering new evidence based on brokers' notices.[6] But Rudkin declined to receive additional evidence from Flagg, denied Flagg's latest motion for a new trial, and sentenced Flagg to 18 months in the federal prison in Atlanta. Flagg was permitted to remain free on $50,000 bail pending appeal.[7] The next day, U.S. District Attorney H. Snowden Marshall dropped all charges against Flagg's alleged co-conspirators, indicating that the preponderance of the testimony taken at Flagg's trial tended to show they were not guilty.[8]

As Flagg and his counsel prepared their appeal over the better part of 1915, Flagg's reputation (or notoriety) went national. In the small Pennsylvania town of Beaver Falls, the Farmers National Bank ran an ad in the local newspaper for ten days straight in mid-January 1915 bearing the headline "52% Flagg" with a caricature of the man himself and his ever-present cigar:[9]

One of the "many people" cited in the ad was Ellsworth E. Cook, who filed a civil complaint against Flagg on August 27, 1915, forcing Flagg to fight his legal battles on two fronts simultaneously.[10] By late December, after at least two long delays in assembling the necessary documents,[11] Flagg decided it was time to change lawyers in his criminal case.[12] Replacing Coleman was Martin W. Littleton of 149 Broadway and his associate Owen N. Brown. They began their representation in January 1916 with an effort to obtain all of the documents filed in connection with the pre-trial motion to recover Flagg's books and papers.

It seems that back on September 26, 1911, three days after the raid on Flagg's offices, when Judge Lacombe ordered the government to show cause why Flagg's books and papers should not be returned, numerous supportive documents were filed in connection with that proceeding. Of particular importance were affidavits from government authorities involved in the raid, including then-D.A. Henry A. Wise, U.S. Marshal

William Henkel, and Postal Inspector Elmer L. Kincaid, which would show that the raid was conducted without proper warrants for the seizure of Flagg's books. Years later, long after the trial, on December 15, 1915, when Brown received the transcript of record, he realized that those documents had not been included.[13]

Littleton wired Judge Rudkin, who had returned to the Eastern District of Washington in Spokane, asking about the documents,[14] then followed up with a lengthy letter detailing the documents in question and stressing their importance to Flagg's pending appeal.[15] In the correspondence that followed, Rudkin said he could not recall whether the affidavits had been formally made a part of the record, but he was "now of the impression that there was no warrant of any kind...." Rudkin said he would do anything he could to make the record conform to the facts as they were presented to him. "[If] the defendant was improperly convicted," he said, "the conviction should not stand."[16]

Armed with Rudkin's recollection, Littleton petitioned the Second Circuit for a writ of certiorari on February 14, 1916.[17] The issue was settled, however, when District Attorney Marshall stipulated that the affidavits of Wise and Henkel could be used in Flagg's appeal without amending the record. Littleton accepted the concession and proceeded to complete his appellate brief.[18]

Littleton's brief for Flagg was filed on February 5, 1916. Littleton's arguments varied little from the arguments made by Coleman in his failed quest for a new trial. The first point—elaborately supported by legal analysis and precedent—urged that the trial court "erred in receiving over defendant's objection evidence of the contents of defendant's books, records and papers which had been unlawfully taken from defendant's possession by officers of the United States Government." The seizure and subsequent admission of this evidence, he wrote, violated Flagg's Fourth and Fifth Amendment rights.[19]

The second argument presented in the brief and extensively documented with Flagg's accounts asserted that there was "no evidence from which the jury could find or infer that the defendant devised a scheme or artifice to defraud."[20] A final argument, only briefly summarized, urged that the trial court erred in "receiving in evidence letters, declarations, written documents and statements of the alleged co-conspirators of the defendant."[21] Littleton completed his brief by declaring that the judgment below should be reversed and a new trial granted.[22]

In his brief for the United States, Marshall began with an exhaustive recitation of the evidence against Flagg. "[T]he evidence conclusively established the guilt of the defendant," Marshall concluded.[23] Marshall then turned to the admissibility of secondary evidence based on the content of Flagg's books, records, and papers. Marshall described the sequence of events through which the evidence was collected, implying that the seizure was legal as incident to Flagg's arrest by New York City municipal police. They "supposed" that Flagg's books and records were "evidence of a crime, in the commission of which Flagg was then and there engaged."[24]

According to Marshall, the authority for the arrest and seizure by the police appeared nowhere in the record of this case, nor did the record show that Flagg was charged with violating any state law or municipal ordinance. Thus, presumably operating on their own initiative, the police took Flagg to the U.S. courthouse where he was arrested by the U.S. Marshal under a warrant issued by Commissioner Gilchrist upon the verified complaint of Post Office Inspector Kincaid charging Flagg with violation of the mail fraud statute. The books and papers were handed over to Post Office Inspector Dickson, Marshall said, emphasizing that the U.S. Marshal never seized or possessed any of Flagg's books or papers.[25]

Nevertheless, Marshall conceded that the books and papers came into the U.S. Attorney's hands—though the record did not show how or when—and were ultimately returned to Flagg. As to the information derived from those materials, Marshall seemed to suggest that poor lawyering on Flagg's behalf allowed the government to retain and, when appropriate, introduce it into evidence.[26]

Turning to the constitutional issues, Marshall argued that, even if the seizure violated the Fourth Amendment, there would be no Fifth Amendment violation unless the defendant himself were called upon to testify about them.[27] He distinguished a U.S. Supreme Court decision, *Boyd v. United States*, that held precisely the opposite,[28] suggesting that subsequent decisions had limited its force.[29] "If the defendant's constitutional rights under the Fourth Amendment were violated by an unlawful search and seizure, the error was cured when the books and records were returned to him on his demand," Marshall asserted, "and the defendant's rights under the Fifth Amendment were not violated...."[30]

Marshall also distinguished the *Weeks* case, which had been asserted below for the proposition that it was reversible error to admit into evidence papers that had been seized without a warrant, even if seized incident to arrest.[31] Among other factual distinctions, Marshall pointed out that all of Flagg's papers were seized by police, not the U.S. Marshal, which the *Weeks* court had held was not a constitutional violation.[32] In any event, Flagg acquiesced in the government's possession of his papers after his original motion to return them was denied.[33]

U.S. Judge Alfred C. Coxe

The following month, the U.S. Court of Appeals for the Second Circuit shredded Marshall's arguments. In an opinion written by Judge Alfred C. Coxe, a three-judge panel of the court asserted that the ultimate fate of Jared Flagg, "important as it is, sinks into insignificance when compared to the right of the people of the United States to be protected from unlawful search."[34]

Coxe recounted the ambiguities in the details of the actual raid on Flagg's offices, finding it "impossible to believe...that the United States, acting through its accredited agents, was not responsible for the arrest of the defendant and the seizure of his property. To attribute such an elaborate and carefully prepared proceeding as was planned to convict the defendant to a few local patrolmen or to some unknown parties, in the face of the fact that the property was immediately carted to the federal courthouse and remained there till the federal officials had obtained all the information desired, makes too severe a demand upon the imagination."[35]

Leaving no doubt that the entry into Flagg's offices and the seizure of his papers were unlawful, and moreover that the federal government had "made or instigated" these misdeeds, Coxe reduced the question before the court to this: "can a party be convicted of a crime upon proof procured from books and papers which have been taken from him by force and without a pretense of legal authority?"[36] To Coxe, the *Boyd* and *Weeks* decisions answered that question conclusively in the negative. "The return of the defendant's books and papers, after all the information contained therein had been obtained by the prosecuting officers, did not cure the trespass," Coxe wrote, calling the return of the documents after three long years "idle ceremony."[37]

Judge Henry G. Ward joined the opinion reversing Flagg's conviction, while Judge Van Vechten Veeder concurred "not in the exercise of my own judgment, but in submission to the authority of the Supreme Court."[38] Even before the official Order for Mandate reversing Flagg's conviction was filed,[39] the Flagg decision was being touted as a valuable legal precedent.[40]

While Flagg was undoubtedly pleased with the outcome—after all, it kept him out of prison—his memoir suggests he was further victimized by the government. "The reversal did not free me," he proclaimed, railing against anyone who might think he "got off on a legal technicality." On the contrary, he wrote, "the Circuit Court Judges did not let me off. They sent my case back to be tried—honestly. And pending said trial they held me under bond—fifty thousand dollars—all of which is a matter of record."[41] It is true that the Order of Mandate from the Second Circuit sent the case back to the District Court with instructions to proceed in accordance with the reversal, in accordance with normal procedure, but the likelihood that the case would be retried was always minimal.

Nevertheless, Flagg's version of the story treats the government's failure to retry him as a further affront. "It was in this last year, 1917, when I stepped forward for [the new trial] that I discovered there would be no trial, he wrote. "If they would have to try me honestly they would not try me at all." Flagg labeled a "subterfuge" Marshall's assertion that he could not be tried because of the Second Circuit ruling. "At the very time he made this excuse to the court my books, as per the Chancery Court files, were on public record in a civil case;[42] and could, therefore, have been subpoenaed and lawfully used by him at a trial…" Instead, Flagg insisted that Marshall declined to retry him because he knew Flagg could disprove "every assertion, every insinuation" made by the government prosecutors.[43]

At the same time, however, Flagg read the Second Circuit opinion as complete vindication:

> My stock brokerage office was not raided by the Government. It was burglarized by officials acting without legal authority and in violation of the law.
>
> My books were not seized by the Government, but stolen by officials acting without legal authority and in violation of the law.
>
> I was not arrested by the Government. I was kidnaped by officials acting without legal authority and in violation of the law.[44]

But that was Flagg writing in 1920. At the time, he had a more pressing problem. That civil case he spoke about was in full swing in another courtroom.

Chapter 7

The Cook Case

Ellsworth E. Cook was a prominent hotelier and sometime entertainer in the town of Shelbyville, Illinois, when he invested some $10,000 with Jared Flagg in three traunches between May 1910 and August 1911. Cook received alleged "profits" of $2,800 on his investment in weekly payments up until the time Flagg's offices were raided in September 1911. By the time Flagg was convicted in November 1914, Cook figured Flagg owed him some $7,000, which he still hadn't received by the following summer.[1] So, on August 27, 1915, Cook filed a lawsuit in U.S. District Court for the Southern District of New York—the same court that had convicted Flagg the previous year—accusing Flagg of defrauding Cook and as many as 600 other investors. The complaint demanded an immediate injunction preventing Flagg from paying out or absconding with any of his fund's assets and the appointment of a temporary receiver.[2]

Gilbert E. Roe

Cook's attorney, Gilbert E. Roe, was a Wall Street lawyer, better known for his legal defense of radical activists such as Emma Goldman and Alexander Berkman, as well as his close personal, political and professional relationship with Wisconsin Sen. Robert La Follette.[3] Roe filed the bill of complaint on behalf of Cook and "all other claimants similarly situated" who cared to join.[4]

Flagg would later write that the Cook lawsuit was instigated, not by Cook, or Roe, or other investors, but by U.S. Attorney H. Snowden Marshall, who was prosecuting the criminal case at the same time. "Mr. Marshall decided it was unwise to permit the Department of Justice to be utilized as a collecting manager," he wrote. "Operations therefore were transferred to the office of Gilbert E. Roe, 55 Liberty Street, who was not an (sic) United States Attorney."[5] The record does not conclusively support Flagg's assertion, but neither does it explain how Cook came to retain Roe in this matter.

In any event, Flagg answered Cook's complaint on September 14 and essentially denied each of the substantive allegations.[6] Specifically, he denied that he owed Cook any money at all, at least until Cook instructed him to close out the positions he held on Cook's behalf. He denied that there were 600 or, indeed any, investors claiming to be in Cook's situation. He denied that he obtained any funds through fraud and misrepresentation, or that payments made to Cook and others were anything but profits on their investments.

Flagg denied that he had "evolved or perfected" the investment scheme that he practiced, but rather asserted that his practices had been successfully used "for generations." He denied the allegation that he never actually bought or sold shares on his clients' behalf and that his brokerage transactions merely offset each other. And he insisted that he followed to the letter the terms of his contracts with Cook and all other investors. Finally, he denied that he appropriated any investor funds for his own use or issued false and misleading letters and circulars to his investors. Flagg also raised a procedural defense, asserting that Cook had an adequate remedy at law, namely a suit for damages, and therefore the court lacked jurisdiction to issue an injunction.[7]

Cook's demands for an immediate injunction and appointment of a receiver were heard by U.S. District Judge Charles M. Hough. Hough was well familiar with Flagg, having overruled Flagg's demurrer to his indictment in 1913.[8] He was also familiar with Cook's lawyer, Gilbert Roe, having ruled against Roe in a libel suit against the muckraking publisher S.S. McClure in 1908.[9] This time, Hough had little difficulty granting Cook's demands. Noting that the

U.S. District Judge Augustus N. Hand

facts charged in Cook's complaint were essentially the same as those charged in Flagg's indictment, Hough declared that his opinion of Flagg's

U.S. District Judge Charles M. Hough

operation had not been changed by his trial. "[By] his conviction, Flagg is presumptively, if not conclusively, held to have done the very things" charged in the bill of complaint and "preliminary relief may be granted by injunction and receiver."[10]

But even without giving any weight to Flagg's conviction, given the pendency of this appeal, Hough said the evidence showed that Flagg "[breached] his agreement with Cook and many others, and, further, that such breach was a calculated one, intended from the beginning." Accordingly, Hough granted Cook's request for injunction and receiver.[11] Four days later, on September 27,

Hough appointed William B. Winslow, who worked out of Roe's office at 55 Liberty Street, as receiver for the funds Flagg had on hand.[12]

Within days, however, on October 7, Roe was back in court asking Judge Augustus Hand for an order requiring Flagg to show cause why he should not be held in contempt for failure to turn over the funds that Winslow was supposed to administer. The proceeding also involved Flagg's brother, Ernest, who posted the $50,000 bond on which Jared was released from custody pending appeal. Apparently, Ernest had never turned over to the receiver the stocks and bonds he held as security for the bail.[13]

Exactly how much money was involved was unclear at this point. It had been estimated that, of the $1.1 million Flagg's operation had taken in, some $200,000[14] or $300,000[15] remained. Through Roe, Winslow reported that, at the time of his arrest, Flagg's bank accounts totaled $154,000, but that he now had less than $20,000 in cash. At the time of the appearance, Winslow had been unable to get into Flagg's safe.[16]

To sort it all out, Hand appointed Wallace MacFarlane as special master, and MacFarlane began taking testimony on November 11, 1915.[17] Roe called Flagg as his first witness and immediately began probing the pyramid-scheme aspects of Flagg's operation—that is, Flagg's efforts to have his existing investors procure new investors in exchange for commissions.[18] Flagg conceded that he had taken in $1,080,000 overall, or 108 of his $10,000 "units."[19] He also acknowledged that, whenever he received a buy order from one customer, he initiated a sell order for the same stock in the same amount for another customer.[20]

Much of Flagg's testimony was taken up with explaining the entries in his various ledgers, but Roe pressed the inconsistencies between stock purchases shown on the ledgers and stocks on hand as reported to the District Attorney at the time of the raid.[21] On cross-examination, Flagg's lawyer, John M. Coleman, elicited an explanation of sorts for the discrepancies and produced a written testimonial on Flagg's behalf from Cook himself.[22] Among others, Roe called Henry D. Mildeberger, Flagg's former head bookkeeper, who spent most of his time on the stand authenticating the books and records that Roe introduced into evidence.[23]

The evidentiary proceedings before the master continued throughout most of 1916. In late May of that year, the U.S. Court of Appeals for the Second Circuit affirmed Judge Hough's decision to appoint a receiver for all of Flagg's funds.[24] While insisting they were not ruling on the merits of the civil case, the judges made clear that they believed Cook's bill stated a viable cause of action in equity and that appointment of a receiver avoided "grave injustice" to prospective claimants.[25] And in early June, Judge Hand granted Roe's motion to take the testimony of many of the claimants by deposition.[26]

The actual trial was scheduled for mid-December 1916, but Flagg decided to take his testimony public—in advance. From December 4 through 10, Flagg held forth every evening at Holland House, Fifth Avenue and 30th Street, at 8:30 p.m., on the subject of "How to Take Money Out of Wall Street," the title of his 1887 book.

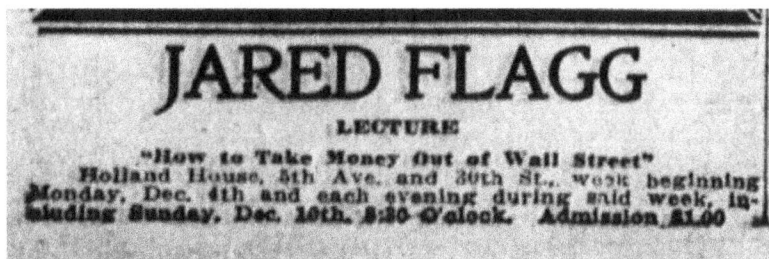

With virtually all of his assets frozen, Flagg also needed to earn some money by selling tickets for $1 each.[27] The *New York Sun* covered the event with tongue firmly in cheek:

> Out of the highways, byways and subways, whither they had been summoned by the glaring advertisement "How to Take Money Out of Wall Street," incipient millionaires to the number of thirty-nine—including four newspaper reporters who got in as deadheads—dissipated the emptiness of the Holland House's ballroom last evening to listen to Jared Flagg. Not only did he tell, but he even demonstrated, a system of money getting as certain as the sun, as unshakable as the axis of the earth....
>
> The audience stopped at the desk of the Holland House on the way out to inquire whether there were any all night

automobile salesrooms and the formalities surrounding yacht charter.[28]

The trial did finally take place before Judge Hand, who heard testimony on December 15, 18 and 19.[29] Flagg was now represented by Philip C. Samuels. Roe's star witness was Flagg's erstwhile book-keeper Henry Mildeberger, whose treachery would later be denounced by Flagg:

> Mr. Roe, retained on a contingent fee, feels that he owes it to himself to make the Court believe [that Flagg defrauded his customers], even if he has to hire a man to commit perjury to convince the court [that the "profits" of $522,145.72 paid to Flagg's customers came from the $1,080,000 in principal that they had paid in]. [It] was due to Mildeberger's testimony that Lawyer Roe was enabled to trick the District Court into deciding against me in my civil case.[30]

And so it did. On May 1, 1917, Judge Hand ruled unequivocally against Flagg.[31] Hand explained Flagg's actual system very clearly. Every buy order from a customer would be offset by a sell order attributed to another customer, such that Flagg held only "trifling" amounts of stock— not nearly enough to cover the alleged holdings of his customers. All of the "profits" paid to those customers came from the funds his customers had invested with him. "The difficulty with defendant's position," Hand said, "is that it is really based upon sophistry, perhaps even of a self-deluded kind.... I find nothing in the contract [with customers], or elsewhere, express or implied, which... relieved him from the ordinary obligation of a broker to a customer purchasing on a margin to have specific securities available to meet his obligations."[32]

On May 9, Hand filed a formal decree, proclaiming that Cook and anyone else who might join the lawsuit, were all entitled to a share of the funds held by the temporary receiver, William Winslow, who would henceforth become permanent. Claims would have to be filed on or before July 16, 1917. Hand ordered Flagg to assign all of the proceeds of his business to Winslow to be held in trust for the claimants. He then went on to list all of the stocks currently held by Winslow and $56,540.63 in cash.

Hand ordered banks, trust companies, surety companies or any other person holding funds or property belonging to Flagg to transfer them to the receiver. Cook was specifically awarded $6,624.12—the difference between his investment and his "profits"—less any amount received from the distribution of Flagg's property among all claimants, though the amount held by the receiver was far less than the total of likely claims. A special master would be appointed to oversee that distribution, along with appropriate compensation and other costs.[33] An advertisement announcing the terms of the receivership was duly published in the *New York Times* on May 19.[34]

Four days later, on May 23, Samuels filed a notice of appeal and assignment of errors on Flagg's behalf with the U.S. Court of Appeals for the Second Circuit.[35] Samuels listed 35 errors—all essentially boiling down to Hand's failure to believe Flagg's assertions—as the basis for his prayer to reverse the judgment and decree and dismiss Cook's complaint.[36] On May 25, Hand ordered Cook to appear before the Second Circuit on June 22, 1917, to show cause why his orders should not be corrected.[37]

Samuels, however, seemed always in need of more time to prepare his case, receiving several extensions through July and August, finally expiring on September 15.[38] Roe apparently had had enough, and on September 22 alerted the Second Circuit that he would soon move to dismiss Flagg's appeal.

> "[T]hroughout the entire proceeding, particularly in taking testimony before the Master, the defendant sought by every device possible, to delay the proceeding. He changed attorneys during said proceeding several times, frequently asked for and secured adjournments because he alleged he was unable to proceed, refused to answer questions propounded to him, although admonished by the Master to answer, and many pages of testimony were frequently taken before the Master in order to get the defendant to answer plain and proper questions, which could have been answered by yes or no, all because of defendant's constant evasions, contradictions and changing of testimony."[39]

Roe provided several pages of transcript to illustrate his point, as well as a letter Flagg sent to his customers boasting of his dilatory tactics.[40] "Five months have now elapsed since this case was decided," Roe concluded, "and about four months since the appeal was taken and we are absolutely no nearer having a record settled than we were the day the appeal was taken.... It has been over two years now since this action was commenced and this trust fund impounded in the Receiver's hands. The defendant has virtually had every contention which he makes in this case passed on three times, twice by the United States District Court and once by this court. It has been held that the facts constituting the fraud in this case not only constitutes fraud but a crime."[41]

Roe's motion to dismiss the appeal and Samuels's opposition to the motion were filed on October 2. "It is always a disagreeable duty to move to dismiss an appeal or take advantage of any default on the part of an adversary," Roe wrote, "and in my opinion, should only be done in a case where it is apparent that the delay or default is intentional or where it is necessary to save the rights of a diligent party or to protect the court from imposition. In the present case, all these considerations seem to me to require that the appeal should be dismissed."[42]

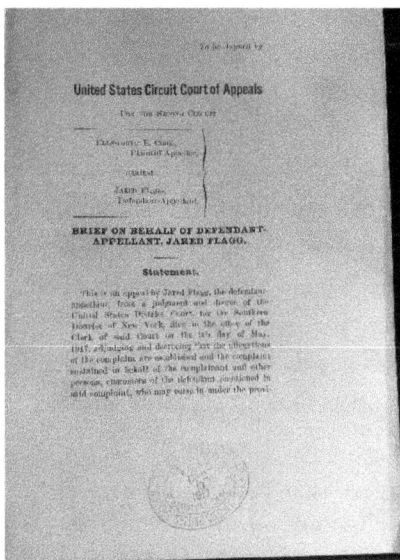

Samuels's response included a deposition by Flagg denying any desire to hinder or delay the appeal, which he insisted was taken in good faith. He also claimed to be puzzled as to why Roe had referred to his operation as a crime, in view of the fact that his conviction had now been reversed and the indictments against him dismissed.[43] On October 15, the court dismissed Roe's motion on the condition that Flagg file the record within thirty days.[44]

Both Samuels and Roe filed appellate briefs on behalf of their respective clients on December 10, 1917. Samuels recounted at length the details of Flagg's investment "system," summarized the testimony and other evidence presented at trial from Flagg's perspective, and argued that the allegations in Cook's complaint had not been sustained. Samuels insisted that all of the business conducted by Flagg under his contracts with Cook was done according to law and demanded that Judge Hand's decree be reversed and the bill of complaint dismissed.[45]

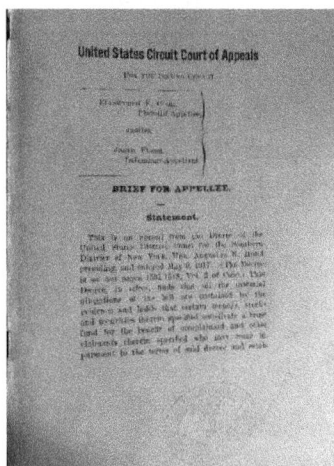

Roe framed his brief in the form of three questions: How much money did Flagg receive from his customers? What did he do with it? What did he tell his customers he would do with their money? A fourth question called for an accounting of the actual transactions in which Flagg engaged under pretense of acting for his customers. The first answer was simple: $1,080,000. The second was more complicated, but it came down to this: $522,000 in "profits" returned to customers; $150,000 net losses with brokers; $54,000 in commissions paid to sales agents; and $280,000 in cash and securities on hand at the time of his arrest. Together with a number of smaller disbursements, this accounted for all the money Flagg took in. "[T]aking these figures exactly as they stand," Roe wrote,

> the foolishness and the falsity of all Flagg's claims respecting his so-called "business" stand revealed. He never added a dollar of profits or an increase, in any form, to the money his customers turned over to him but actually lost over One hundred fifty thousand dollars of their money and returned back to them over half a million dollars of their own money cunningly paid each week to beguile others into the business and falsely called the amounts so returned "profits." Other large amounts were paid out to agents for the purpose of bringing in additional victims. These are the facts with regard to Flagg's "business" and show it to be nothing more than a colossal and cleverly devised and an adroitly concealed swindle.[46]

As to Flagg's representations to his customers, Roe pointed to the various letters, circulars, advertisements and books that Flagg had promulgated over the years. All of them, in one way or another, touted Flagg's supposed system of buying stocks when they dropped a point and selling only when they gained a point.[47] The actual transactions however, were merely offsetting purchases and sales of the same stocks that left Flagg's position unchanged, except for the net transactional losses he incurred.[48] Following a brief review of the applicable law,[49] Roe asked that the decree be affirmed.[50]

The case was heard on December 11, 1917, by a three-judge panel of the Second Circuit court consisting of Circuit Judge Henry Wade Rogers and District Judges Julius M. Mayer and Learned Hand, cousin of trial judge Augustus N. Hand. Learned Hand, who wrote the opinion, did not always agree with his cousin, on law or politics,[51] but this time the two jurists were utterly in synch, and the appellate court affirmed the decree with costs.[52]

Judge Henry Wade Rogers

Learned Hand's opinion consisted of a restatement of the facts as shown at the trial and an elaborate hypothetical demonstrating a fairly simple point. Flagg's way of doing business—offsetting every purchase with an immediate sale—deprived his investors of any property right in the securities they asked him to purchase. However the investor's interests

Judge Julius M. Mayer

might have appeared to be protected by contractual arrangements, Hand wrote, he would have no claim to the shares his investment purportedly purchased. Should Flagg become insolvent, his investors would have no recourse whatsoever. Twice before in Massachusetts and once in the Seventh Circuit, courts held that, in similar circumstances, the defrauded investor could recover from the broker.[53]

Flagg filed motions for a rehearing on January 26 and again on February 18, both times arguing that the court erred in accepting as fact Cook's principal allegation, namely that Flagg's offsetting transactions meant that "no stock was actually bought or sold for any customer, and the purchases and sales were a fiction and pretense on [Flagg's] part." In the first, apparently prepared by attorney John M. Coleman, Flagg conceded that, had this actually occurred, he would have been guilty of illegal "bucketing," but insisted that the only "evidence" to substantiate this contention was the assertion of Gilbert Roe.[54] The second, which bears only Flagg's name, focused more on the courts' failure to understand the beauty of his system and the wisdom of his investors.[55]

Neither motion succeeded. On February 26, 1918, the court issued its order for mandate affirming the district court's decree.[56] Flagg's petition to the United States Supreme Court to review his case was denied a little over two months later.[57] Meanwhile, Flagg had already moved on to his next venture, a real estate business,[58] leasing offices at 15–17 East 40th Street.[59] Ellsworth Cook lived until 1924, having sold his hotel the previous year due to failing health.[60]

Chapter 8

Final Years

A. The Crimes of Jared Flagg

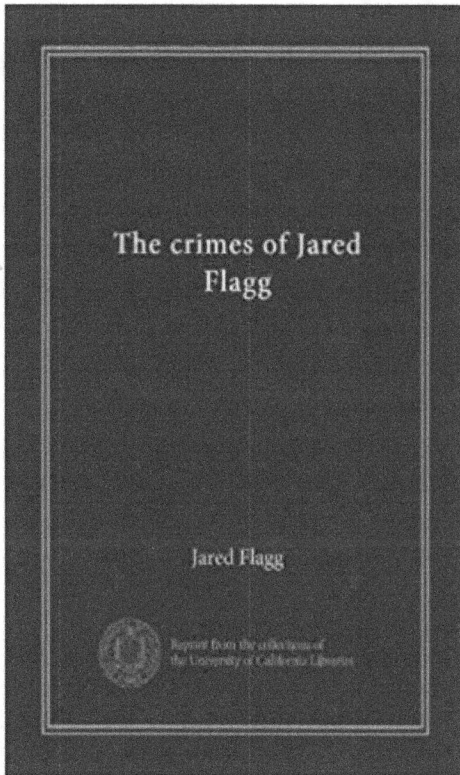

Two projects seem to have occupied Jared Flagg following his conclusive defeat at the hands of Ellsworth Cook and Gilbert Roe: writing his book, *The Crimes of Jared Flagg*, and returning to the real estate business. The book actually began much earlier, with *Flagg's Flats*, a monograph about Flagg's war with the New York City Police Department, written in 1907. "No publisher would accept the manuscript," Flagg would write in an introduction to *Crimes*, "fearing he might become implicated legally. A few typewritten copies were read by my friends all of whom advised me not to have it published on the ground that it might cost me my life."[1]

At the time, Flagg wrote, "I was recklessly indifferent. Nothing cuts deeper than undeserved slander and I had been cut to the quick." Flagg finally found a printer, Charles Francis, who agreed to publish the book—after his lawyer had time to examine the court records to verify its truthfulness—and the first edition came out in 1908. "Seven editions followed," Flagg reported, "each larger than the preceding one."[2]

Several of those editions are available today in various digitized and print-on-demand forms. One of them, carrying a copyright date of 1909, contains a preface in which Flagg denies any attempt to "palliate my own faults and make my side appear better, or the other side appear worse, than the facts justify." Rather, he wrote, it is a "simple narrative" based on the court records, instead of the "six hundred and forty-five 'fairy tales' circulated about me; only six hundred and forty-five newspaper articles, which were highly colored and misleading."[3]

This particular edition of *Flats*, called *Flats I* herein, retrieved from Google Books, was digitized from the collection of the University of Michigan Library and is inscribed "The Gift of Mr. Jared Flagg."[4] A presumably later edition, a reprint by Forgotten Books, carries a series of requests for copies from university libraries all over the country, including this from Michigan:

> We have five copies of your book, "Flagg's Flats." If you can spare another copy it would be much appreciated by the following: Miss Mary Pratt, Librarian, Mitchell Public Library, Hillsdale, Mich. Please send C.O.D. direct to Hillsdale.
>
> Thanking you for your kind response to our former request, I am
>
> Very gratefully yours,
Theo. W. Koch,
Librarian[5]

Bartow S. Weeks

This edition also contains a message for the newspaper editors Flagg held responsible for the "fairy tales" mentioned in his earlier preface. Pointing out that libel could be a criminal offense, Flagg said he sent marked copies of the book to all of them, as well as certain public officials, accusing them of being "liars and scoundrels and thieves and blackmailers and perjurers and forgers" and waited to see what they would do about it. "They didn't do anything. They didn't even let out a peep," he wrote, implying that he would surely have been charged with criminal libel if anything he wrote in the book was false.[6]

In 1912, "incensed beyond endurance" following his arrest and the raid on his offices in September 1911, Flagg published *Flats* in combination with an early account of the raid, calling the work, *The Flagg Raid*. "In this one hundred-and-seven-page booklet," he wrote later, "I told [the U.S. Attorneys] what I thought of them and their methods of dispensing injustice. I also told [Assistant U.S. Attorney Claude A.] Thompson what I thought of him and his method of investigating himself."[7]

Flagg claimed that the Charles Francis Press printed 62,000 copies of *Raid*, distributed at the rate of 5,000 copies a day. "One was mailed to every lawyer in Greater New York and Washington, D.C.," Flagg would write. "Also to every postmaster, congressman, senator, and high office holder in the United States. Many copies were sold on news stands, especially at the Park Row Building, in which the offices of Claude A. Thompson were located...."[8]

In 1917, after Flagg's conviction was overturned and while his appeal in the *Cook* case was pending, Flagg cobbled together a third book, *The Crimes of Jared Flagg*, comprising *Flats* as Part I and an updated *Raid* as Part II. Two very distinct version of *Crimes* are readily available today, although both bear the copyright date of 1920. Indeed, *Crimes* appears on the 1920 copyright register published in April of that year.[9] One of the two versions runs to about 350 pages,[10] the other around 200.[11] While there is no definitive way to tell which was written first, internal evidence suggests that the longer version (*Crimes I*) was rigorously edited down to the more manageable one (*Crimes II*).

There are some substantive differences between Part I of *Crimes I* and *II*. *Crimes I*, for example, like the stand-alone versions of *Flats*, contains a diatribe against one Bartow S. Weeks, an assistant to then-New York City District Attorney Col. John R. Fellows, who had been a bookkeeper for Flagg when he was in the wholesale fish business. "This young man Weeks, it appears, entertained a secret grudge against me," Flagg wrote. "He worked against me as he had never worked for me, and with all the venom, hate and malice of a disgruntled and discharged employee...."[12] This entire episode is missing from *Crimes II*.

Both Part I of *Crimes I* and *Flats* also contain a lengthy condemnation of Flagg's landlord at the Century Building, 1 West 34th Street, where he leased office space in 1908, for various perceived slights and injustices as a consequence of Flagg's growing notoriety. Based on the "unanimous wish of the majority of the tenants...that I should be put out of the building," Flagg wrote, "Minturn Post Collins—the man whose word was supposed to be as good as his bond—broke his word and refused to rent to me or my partners the two additional offices he had previously agreed to do."[13] That, too, disappeared from *Crimes II*.

Also edited out of Part I of *Crimes II* was a long, fictional courtroom examination, in which Flagg lampooned his own theatrical license renewal fiasco.[14] Otherwise, Part I of *Crimes II* seems like a more tightly edited version of Part I of *Crimes I* and *Flats*. In contrast, the changes in Part II from *Crimes I* to *Crimes II* seem much more significant. For example, Flagg initially quoted an entire *New York Herald* article written sarcastically about his move to the Century Building and the stock scheme he promoted;[15] only the headline appears in the later version.[16]

Only *Crimes I* contains an attack on "Germans who secretly sympathize with Germany, all of whom, in my opinion, should be dumped into garbage scows, and made to tow themselves back to their 'Fatherland.'"[17] This is the only place in all of Flagg's writings that reveal a sense of the world beyond New York City and his own predicaments. *Crimes I* also contains rather more detail on Flagg's stormy relationship with the *New York World*, including the charge that the reporter covering the raid on his offices, a Mrs. Rand, won a $100 prize from the paper for turning in the most sensational story.[18]

Crimes I also includes a bit of self-reflection concerning the wisdom of Flagg's circulating the pamphlet *Flagg's Raid*. "Many persons say I made a mistake in writing this pamphlet. Possibly I did—I do not know—but what of it? A man who never made a mistake never made anything."[19] *Crimes II* entertains no such doubts. Moreover, about one and a half chapters in *Crimes I*, containing a focused attack on Assistant U.S. Attorney Thompson, is left out of *Crimes II* altogether.[20]

Perhaps the most striking difference between the two versions is the total omission from *Crimes II* of any mention of the *Cook* civil case. The last chapter of *Crimes I* rails at the entire proceeding as a sham invented by Thompson and Cook's lawyer, Gilbert Roe, and Roe's star witness, Flagg's own book-keeper (and erstwhile lawyer), Henry Mildeberger. In October 1917, six months after the district court's ruling in *Cook*, "and long after Mildeberger had sold himself to Lawyer Roe, he called at my stock brokerage house, 90 Wall Street, New York City, to sell himself to me—for a position. He did not procure the position…"[21] Flagg included an affidavit from the supposedly remorseful Mildeberger denying that the profits paid to Flagg's customers came from their own investments.[22]

The concluding portions of the two versions differ largely in organization, though a lot of repetitive language was edited out of *Crimes*

II. But both versions of Jared Flagg's magnum opus end with a variant of the phrase:

And,

such were

THE "CRIMES" OF JARED FLAGG[23]

B. Flagg's Last Scam

In 1917, the year Flagg completed at least the first draft of *Crimes*, he incorporated The Jared Flagg Corporation in New York City,[24] with himself as president and treasurer and Henry A. Jackson, a stockbroker crony of Flagg's from the old Jared Flagg Co.,[25] as secretary. For the next three years, Flagg said later, he remained in the brokerage business,[26] although he must have maintained a low profile given the nearly total absence of newspaper coverage between the conclusion of the *Cook* case and 1920. The 1920 Census shows Flagg living with one Edna W. Baumann, a thirty-year-old nurse from New Jersey, whom Flagg falsely identified as a cousin.[27]

In August 1920, the New York newspapers reported the purchase of the former residence of one William D. Baldwin at 14 West 68th Street, adjoining the Second Church of Christ Scientist, at the southwest corner of 68th and Central Park West. The four-story building stood on a lot measuring 50 x 100.5 feet, and the selling price was listed at $83,000. The seller was Walter Russell, Penrhyn Stanlaws, and Associates, owners of the adjacent Hotel des Artistes, 1 West 67th Street, who had bought the property in February 1919. The new owner of record was The Jared Flagg Corporation, with management by a 14 West 68th Street Corporation, newly incorporated by Jackson, Madeline Russe, Flagg's former confidential secretary, and one J. W. Moller.[28] The Flagg Corporation would soon move its offices from 15 East 40th Street to that building.[29]

The Jared Flagg Corporation also owned an adjacent twenty-five-foot lot at 12 West 68th Street, and the two parcels effectively became one, known as 12–14 West 68th Street. In August 1921, plans were filed by the corporation through its architect, Jared's brother Ernest, to build another four-story building there,[30] but apparently nothing came of the project.

Jared Flagg seems to have found another way to profit from the properties—Flagg's last scam.

By late 1921, the Flagg Corporation property at 12–14 West 68th was encumbered by mortgages totaling about $65,000.[31] The record does not show whether Flagg was having difficulty paying his monthly mortgage bill or whether he simply wanted to increase his profits from the property.[32] In any event, Flagg began distributing a series of circulars advertising—in true Jared Flagg fashion:

The Only Logical Solution of the

RENT PROBLEM

Conceived by
JARED FLAGG

(6% Guaranteed Profit-Participation Bonds)[33]

The bonds, which Flagg would sell at $100 each, to his own tenants and to others, were guaranteed to pay 6% interest per year, payable at 0.5% a month. The bonds would also pay holders a share of the profits from the property, if any, up to another 6% per year. The corporation could call in the bonds at any time, with ninety days' notice, paying the holders $100 in gold coins.[34]

The circulars contained a typical Flagg sales pitch, partly in question-and-answer format, explaining how the extra income from the bonds could reduce tenants' rental costs. "It is not so much the guaranteed interest as it is the unguaranteed profit," one of Flagg's circulars proclaimed. "Therein lies the solution." They also explained how the bonds were secured—or supposedly secured.[35]

On November 1, 1921, Flagg issued the first of these bonds, in a series of 400, which he promised to secure by placing a $40,000 mortgage on the land and improvements, subject to the original $65,000 obligation, to run for a term of ten years beginning January 1, 1922.[36] The corporation actually secured a mortgage for only $20,000—not $40,000—and recorded it on April 19, 1922. The mortgage provided that the entire principal amount would become due and payable to Jared Flagg and Henry

A. Jackson—now in their capacity as trustees for the bondholders—upon a default in the payment of any installment of principal or interest for twenty days.[37]

No interest was ever paid on the bonds.

Without authorization from the bondholders, Flagg borrowed additional funds against the property from the West Side Savings Bank and other individual lenders, entering into a variety of agreements with them that subordinated the bondholders' interests to these new liens. In 1926, the bondholders filed a civil lawsuit against The Jared Flagg Corporation and the other banks and individual lenders to foreclose two mortgages: the $20,000 recorded mortgage, as well as a $40,000 "equitable" mortgage based on Flagg's representations. The mortgage lenders, in turn, counterclaimed that, no matter what might have been due the bondholders on account of the default, their claims were superior because of the subordination agreements they had from Flagg.[38]

Albert E. Ottinger

On August 26, 1926, Flagg was summoned to the Manhattan Life Building offices of New York Attorney General Albert Ottinger's Bureau for the Prevention and Punishment of Fraud[39] under a provision of state law known as the Martin Act[40] authorizing the Bureau to investigate the "issuance, sale and negotiation of securities" in the state.[41] Also present was J.W. Kaufman, attorney for the bondholders.

Deputy Attorney General Keyes Winter questioned Flagg extensively about the 68th Street bonds. Flagg—who was now the sole trustee for the bondholders, Henry Jackson having passed away earlier[42]— testified that he believed the bondholders' claims had priority over claims of the later mortgage holders on the ground that he received the money from them earlier. Winter challenged that assertion, but Flagg gave no response. Later, Winter would testify as a witness in the civil suit:

> Q. Isn't it a fact that [Flagg] became unconscious while he was actually being examined there?
>
> A. He became unconscious right after I concluded the examination. I had one more question that I put to him, and then he commenced to choke and lost his hold of himself.
>
> Q. And he never answered it?
>
> A. He never answered that question.[43]

Winter called for a doctor, but Jared Flagg was dead of an apparent heart attack when the doctor arrived. On Flagg's death, Kaufman was appointed successor trustee for the bondholders and the case went to trial.[44] In his opinion, New York Supreme Court Justice Jeremiah T. Mahoney called Flagg "quite an undesirable person and a man of bad character and reputation." Mahoney ruled that Flagg's testimony before the Attorney General was inadmissible:

> I have decided to give no credence or weight to the declarations attributed to him. Even if I should have decided his declarations were competent proof I would have given practically no weight and credence to them because in view of the character of the man as disclosed by the evidence he was a most unreliable person and I have reached the conclusion that his examination before the attorney-general was more or less influenced by the fear that he was in trouble and he apparently made statements that might have the effect of staying any criminal prosecution against him.[45]

Mahoney held that the mortgage lenders had priority over the bondholders. Flagg's old nemesis, Gilbert Roe, joined with Kaufman in appealing the decision. Before the Appellate Division, the bondholders fared a little better, winning priority with respect to the $20,000 recorded mortgage. In his opinion, Justice James O'Malley held that the lenders failed to meet their burden to prove that Flagg had the authority to execute valid subordination agreements with respect to that mortgage. As to the equitable mortgage, however, the court agreed with Justice Mahoney that the lenders had priority as innocent third parties in Flagg's "unscrupulous"[46] and "derelict[ ]" transactions.[47]

Perhaps the unkindest postmortem cut of all came from Jared's favorite brother Ernest. According to papers filed in Surrogate's Court on September 4, 1926, Jared Flagg died with only $65,000 to his name.[48] He had never married, but in the year before his death, he was living with a twenty-year-old woman named Minifred Barry, claiming to be her sole boarder.[49] Whatever their relationship, Jared bequeathed his entire estate to Ernest and named him executor.[50] Ernest, who had supported Jared throughout his checkered career, refused the honor.[51]

Following a funeral at Madison Avenue's Frank E. Campbell Funeral Chapel, Flagg's remains were cremated and his ashes buried with other family members at Evergreen Cemetery in New Haven.[52]

Jared Bradley Flagg

C. Epilogue

Exactly what made Jared Flagg turn to the dark side is best left to psychologists or psychiatrists, but one can speculate that the challenge of living up to the accomplishments of his immediate family played some role in his development.

When Jared Bradley Flagg died in his New York home at age eighty in 1899, his obituary appeared in newspapers throughout the East and Midwest.[53] Perhaps the most elaborate of these appeared in the *Hartford Courant*, which carried a line drawing of the highly regarded artist. That was hardly surprising, given the Flaggs' close association with New Haven and Charles Noël Flagg's residence in Hartford. "Mr. Flagg had a high reputation in portraiture," the article said. "His ideal pieces express refinement, good taste, a faithful feeling for color, and are invariably pleasing.... Among the more notable of Mr. Flagg's portraits were several judges of the New York court of appeals, a full-length picture of William M. Evarts,[54] and several of Commodore Vanderbilt."[55]

Montague Flagg

Jared Bradley's eldest son, Montague Flagg, died in 1915 of pneumonia at age seventy-three following an illness of several weeks' duration. Montague was born in Hartford, and the *Courant* again carried a lengthy obituary. After trying his hand at business in Australia, Montague returned to Hartford in 1882 and to the family's artistic tradition. "He was a modest and very critical artist," the newspaper reported, "working slowly and carefully, and never allowing a canvas to leave his studio until it was as good as he could make it." With his half-brother, Charles Noël, and a friend, Montague studied with Louis Jacquesson de la Chevreuse in Paris, where he was joined by his wife, the former Elise Cordier. Montague exhibited a portrait of Charles Foster of Farmington, Connecticut, in the Paris Salon in 1878, and won the silver medal at the St. Louis Exposition in 1904. Other notable portraits included one of his brother-in-law, Charles Scribner, his sister-in-law, Mrs. Charles Noël Flagg, and members of the Cornelius Vanderbilt family.[56]

Charles Noël Flagg

Charles Noël died almost a year after Montague, on November 10, 1916, age sixty-eight, apparently of heart disease. Having followed Montague to Paris, he returned to found the Connecticut League of Art Students in Hartford and, like his father and older brother, belonged to many of the leading art societies. He won the Thomas R. Proctor prize for a portrait in the National Academy of Design Exhibition in 1908, and wrote a book on "The Evolution of an Equestrian Statue."[57] Charles Noël married the former Ellen F. Earle in 1874, but may have had a roving eye. In 1889, at age fifty-one, he was sued by a Mr. Neil McLeod Keating seeking $50,000 for the alienation of the affections of Keating's wife.[58] Charles Noël Flagg's papers can be found in the Archives of American Art, Smithsonian Institution.

As accomplished as the two eldest brothers were, Ernest was by far the most famous, and controversial, of all of Jared Flagg's siblings. Among his many accomplishments were the design of the Corcoran Gallery of Art in Washington, D.C., 1892–97, the Singer Building in New York City, 1896–98, and the United States Naval Academy in Annapolis, Md., 1900. Born four years after Jared, Ernest remained steadfastly loyal to his older brother throughout his career, but he paid a price. As his biographer, Mardges Bacon, put it:

There is little doubt that the architectural community, especially in New York, mistrusted [Ernest], however much they admired his "capacity and talent." From the time that Ernest, his father, and [Jared Jr.] were engaged in speculative building in New York during the 1880s, they were decidedly controversial. Then, in the midst of the Corcoran affair[59] in 1896, family difficulties added to [Ernest's] own. Jared, his favorite brother, was arrested for running a house of prostitution by renting what were euphemistically called "furnished flats." But Jared's term of thirty days in the Tombs did not dissuade him from future brushes with the law in which he vehemently proclaimed his innocence. On the one hand [Ernest's] early business association with Jared undoubtedly

Ernest Flagg

encouraged his shrewdness. On the other hand, Jared's troubles may have injured further [Ernest's] reputation.[60]

Ernest Flagg died in 1947 at age ninety. His papers are available in Avery Drawings and Archives, Avery Architectural and Fine Arts Library, Columbia University.

Washington Allston Flagg, fifth son of Jared Bradley, was a founding partner in the Wall Street brokerage of Post & Flagg, along with George B. Post, Jr. Founded in 1888, the firm survived well into the 20th Century, with offices throughout the United States, as well as in Montreal and London, under the leadership of W.A. Flagg, Jr. During his lifetime, Flagg was director of the Robins Conveying Belt Company and a member of several riding, golf, tennis and social clubs in New York and New Jersey. The family was mentioned frequently in the society columns and sports pages of the New

W. ALLSTON FLAGG
POST & FLAGG

Washington Allston Flagg

York newspapers.[61] Flagg died in 1903, leaving a wife, the former Anna D. Robins, and three children.[62]

Louise Flagg Scribner

As might be expected for the times, Flagg's nearest sister, Louise, was better known for her marriage to the publisher Charles Scribner II than for her own accomplishments. Scribner died in 1930 in New York City at age seventy-six.[63] Louise Flagg Scribner died in 1948 at age eighty-six in Morristown, N.J.,[64] leaving her daughter and sister Rosalie.

Rosalie's mother, Louisa Hart Flagg, died ten weeks after Rosalie's birth in 1866, so she was raised in part by her uncle and aunt, William J. and Eliza Longworth Flagg. Rosalie married William Dexter Jaffray in 1890, and the couple lived alternately in Manhattan and Nantucket. Rosalie's principal claim to fame seems to have been her membership in Mrs. Astor's storied Four Hundred socialites.[65] Family lore has it that the couple was "mildly eccentric"; both died in 1949.[66]

Rosalie Flagg Jaffray

Jared Flagg, Jr., is largely forgotten today. Even Flagg family members who take great and justifiable pride in their genealogy don't know much about him. "His niece/my grandmother Marion Flagg Maxson (1887–1972) thought he was a rascal and spoke very little of him," wrote architectural historian Peter Flagg Maxson, "and it was only when a cousin happened on *The Crimes of Jared Flagg* in a used bookstore that the rest of the family learned much."[67]

Rascal he was, and then some.

Selected Bibliography

Bacon, Mardges. *Ernest Flagg: Beaux-Arts Architect and Urban Reformer*. Cambridge: MIT Press, 1986.

Bernstein, Rachel Amelia. *Boarding-House Keepers and Brothel Keepers in New York City 1880–1910*. Unpublished Ph.D. dissertation, Rutgers University, 1984.

Burrows, Edwin G. & Mike Wallace. *Gotham: A History of New York City to 1898*. New York: Oxford University Press, 1999.

Czitrom, Daniel. *New York Exposed: The Gilded Age Police Scandal That Launched the Progressive Era*. New York: Oxford University Press, 2016.

Easton, Eric B. *Defending the Masses: A Progressive Lawyer's Battles for Free Speech*. Madison: University of Wisconsin Press, 2018.

Flagg, Ernest. "A Fish Story: An Autobiographical Sketch of the Education of an Architect." *Journal of American Institute of Architects* 3 (May 1945): 182-188.

Flagg, Ernest. *Flagg's Small Houses, Their Economic Design and Construction*. Mineola, N.Y.: Dover Publications, Inc., 1922.

Flagg, Ernest. *Genealogical Notes on the Founding of New England*. Hartford: Case, Lockwood & Brainard Co., 1926.

Flagg, Ernest. *The Works of Ernest Flagg*. New York: The Architectural Record Co., 1902.

Flagg, Norman Gershom. *Family Records of the Descendants of Gershom Flagg*. Moro, Ill.: Norman Gershom Flagg & Lucius C.S. Flagg, 1907.

Flagg, Jared. *Flagg's Flats*. New York: Charles Francis Press, 1908.

Flagg, Jared. *The Crimes of Jared Flagg*. New York: Jared Flagg, 1920.

Flagg, Jared. *The Flagg Raid*. New York: Charles Francis Press, 1912.

Gunther, Gerald. *Learned Hand: The Man and the Judge.* New York: Alfred A. Knopf, 1994.

Leadon, Fran. *Broadway.* New York: W. W. Norton & Co., 2018.

Maxson, Peter Flagg. "Some Descendants of Thomas Flegg (1615-1698)." *Austin Genealogical Soc'y Q.* 36 (1995): 60 (1995), http://www.austintxgensoc.org/wp-content/uploads/2012/04/1995.2.pdf.

Miller,William. "The Original Schemer." *Time*, March 7, 2012.

Report of the Special Committee Appointed to Investigate the Police Department of the City of New York, S. Rep. No. 25, (N.Y. 1895) (Lexow Committee Report).

Tichi, Cecelia. *What Would Mrs. Astor Do?* New York: Washington Mews Books, 2018.

"Trading on a Scale: Is There a Safe Method of Operating on This Plan?" *The Ticker and Investment Digest* 5, no. 4 (February 1910): 170.

Wallace, Mike. *Greater Gotham: A History of New York from 1898 to 1919.* New York: Oxford University Press, 2017.

Wyckoff, Richard D. "Looking Forward—and Backward After Thirty-Five Years in Wall Street." *The Magazine of Wall Street* 33, no. 4 (December 22, 1923): 298.

Endnotes

Notes to Chapter 1

[1] JEFFREY A. KROESSLER, NEW YORK YEAR BY YEAR 205 (2002).

[2] *66 Broadway Sold; Long a Landmark*, N.Y. TIMES, Feb. 18, 1928, at 29.

[3] The Bureau was created to carry out the mandate of the state legislature to investigate fraud in the sale and circulation of bonds, stock certificates and other securities. Laws of 1921, ch. 649; *see In re* Ottinger, 148 N.E. 627 (N.Y. 1926).

[4] *Jared Flagg, 70, Dies at Inquiry*, N.Y. DAILY NEWS, Aug. 27, 1926, 46; "Jared Flagg, Who Promised Many Elmirans Big Profit, Dies While Being Quizzed," STAR-GAZETTE (Elmira, N.Y.), Aug. 27, 1926, at 16. While both newspapers put Flagg's age at 70, he was actually 73.

[5] *File Will of Broker Who Died on Grill*, DAILY EAGLE (Brooklyn, N.Y.), Sept. 12, 1923, at 22.

[6] MARDGES BACON, ERNEST FLAGG: BEAUX-ARTS ARCHITECT AND URBAN REFORMER 6–9 (1986).

[7] *Id.*

[8] *Post & Flagg and Gray & Wilmerding Will Merge Under Former's Name on Jan. 1,* N.Y. TIMES, Dec. 30, 1938, 24.

[9] BACON, *supra* note 6, 9.

[10] Peter Flagg Maxson, *Some Descendants of Thomas Flegg (1615–1698),* 36 AUSTIN GENEALOGICAL SOC'Y Q. 60 (1995), http://www.austintxgensoc.org/wp-content/uploads/2012/04/1995.2.pdf.

[11] Kaufman v. The Jared Flagg Corp., 237 N.Y.S. 26 (App. Div. 1929). *See infra* ch. 8 for analysis of that case.

[12] *See, e.g., Igel Attorneys Plan to Use Flagg Ruling,* N.Y. TRIBUNE, May 12, 1916, 4; *Von Igel Will Fight to Get Papers Back,* N.Y. SUN, May 12, 1916, 5; *Lyman Feels Hurt by Ugly Indictment—May Try Jared Flagg Plea,* N.Y. TIMES, June 1, 1916, 24; *Whitman Acts in Swann Case,* N.Y. HERALD, Jan. 16, 1917, at

1; *Swann Gives Up Hope of Inquiry Into Oil Frauds,* N.Y. TRIBUNE, May 28, 1919, 20; *Newman Will Tell Jury of Oil Deals, N.Y. HERALD*, June 8, 1919, 6.

[13] JARED FLAGG, THE CRIMES OF JARED FLAGG 155-56 (1920)[hereinafter CRIMES II]. Part I of this book was first published under the name FLAGG'S FLATS in 1908. Part II, which was added in 1917, had previously been published under the name THE FLAGG RAID in 1912. There are at least two separate versions of CRIMES, both of which bear a 1920 copyright date. The version that I have labeled CRIMES II, and have relied on for the first six chapters, is a reprint by the Leopold Classic Library, http://www.leopoldclassiclibrary.com. The version cited in chapters 7 and 8, labeled CRIMES I because it appears to be the earlier of the two, is available at http://www.archive.org/details/crimesofjared00flag and the UCLA Library. For a more complete explanation, see *infra* ch. 8. Although I have used all the Flagg books as references throughout this biography, I have tried to approach them with all the skepticism they deserve.

[14] Maxson, *supra* note 10, at 61.

[15] *Id.* at 60; email from Peter Flagg Maxson, on file with author. Eighteenth Century Flagg family portraits, which hung for many years in the billiards room of The Breakers are now housed in the historic Redwood Library in Newport.

[16] ERNEST FLAGG, GENEALOGICAL NOTES ON THE FOUNDING OF NEW ENGLAND 135 (1926); NORMAN GERSHOM FLAGG, FAMILY RECORDS OF THE DESCENDANTS OF GERSHOM FLAGG 125 (1907).

[17] Ernest Flagg, *A Fish Story: An Autobiographical Sketch of the Education of an Architect,* 3 J. AM. INSTITUTE OF ARCHITECTS 182 (1945).

[18] BACON, *supra* note 6, 9.

[19] Email from Peter Flagg Maxson, *supra* note 15.

[20] CRIMES II, *supra* note 13, 155–56.

[21] *Id.* at 156.

[22] EDWIN G. BURROWS & MIKE WALLACE, GOTHAM: A HISTORY OF NEW YORK CITY TO 1898 914 (1999).

[23] *A Fish Story, supra* note 17, 182–83.

[24] Email from Peter Flagg Maxson, *supra* note 15.

[25] *A Fish Story, supra* note 17, 185.

[26] Jared Flagg—Cross Examination, in Transcript of Record, Cook v. Flagg, 251 F. 5 (2d Cir. 1918) (No. 297), on file at National Archives & Records Administration, Kansas City, Mo., Case File No. 6205, at 555.

[27] Untitled, BROOKLYN DAILY EAGLE, March 9, 1881, at 2.

[28] *Business Embarrassments*, N.Y. TIMES, March 9, 1881, 8.

[29] *Big Prices for Real Estate, N.Y. SUN*, Dec. 28, 1882, 2.

[30] Christopher Gray, *The Plazas That Predate the Plaza*, N.Y. TIMES, Aug. 21, 2005, sec. 11, at 8.

[31] Jared Flagg, Jr., *In Court Again*, N.Y. EVENING WORLD, June 11, 1895, at 8. The term "bucket shop" refers to an office with facilities for making bets in the form of orders or options based on current exchange prices of securities or commodities, but without any actual buying or selling of the property. *Peter J. M'Coy, 70, Former U.S. Aide*, N.Y. TIMES, July 19, 1958, at 15.

[32] *Lecture by Jared Flagg*, BROOKLYN DAILY EAGLE, June 16, 1864, at 3.

[33] Letters Patent No. 80,720 (filed Aug. 4, 1868).

[34] *See* Kathy Greer, *Glass Fire Extinguishers Can Be Hazardous To Your Health!* (2007), Rick's Bottle Room.Com, https://poisonsnmore.webs.com/firegrenade hazards.htm.

[35] Advertisement, SALT LAKE HERALD, March 25, 1885, at 7.

[36] *Hand Grenade Notice*, NEW HAVEN DAILY MORNING JOURNAL & COURIER, April 8, 1885, at 3.

[37] *Honorably Discharged*, BROOKLYN DAILY EAGLE, March 26, 1885, at 2.

[38] Advertisement, WEEKLY ARIZONA MINER, June 5, 1885, at 3.

[39] *New Buildings*, NEW HAVEN DAILY MORNING JOURNAL & COURIER, Aug. 29, 1885, at 2.

[40] *Court Notes*, NEW HAVEN DAILY MORNING JOURNAL & COURIER, Oct. 13, 1885, at 3.

[41] *The Court Record*, NEW HAVEN DAILY MORNING JOURNAL & COURIER, Feb. 10, 1886, at 2; Mar. 2. 1886, at 4.

[42] *The Court Record*, NEW HAVEN DAILY MORNING JOURNAL & COURIER, June 17, 1886, at 4.

[43] *The Court Record*, NEW HAVEN DAILY MORNING JOURNAL & COURIER, Feb. 4, 1887, at 4; Feb. 19, 1887, at 4.

[44] *Jared Flagg, Jr., in Court Again*, N.Y. EVENING WORLD, June 11, 1895, at 8.

[45] THE FLAGG RAID, *supra* note 13, at 6. *See infra* ch. 8 for more information on this book.

[46] Bissell v. Press Pub. Co., 17 N.Y.S. 393 (Sup. Ct. 1891).

---

[47] Complaint at 4, Bissell v. Press Pub. Co., 17 N.Y.S. 393 (Sup. Ct. 1891) (citing *Bissell is in the Tombs. The Swindler Twice Exposed by "The World" Arrested Yesterday*, N.Y. WORLD, July 29, 1888), available in Papers on Appeal, https://play.google.com/books/reader?id=ssprCMF7CO0C&hl=en&pg=GBS.PP3.

[48] Complaint, *supra* note 47, at 3 (citing unnamed article in N.Y. WORLD, Aug. 1, 1888).

[49] *Id.* at 5-6 (citing *Bissell is in the Tombs, supra* note 43).

[50] *Id.* at 7-8 (citing *Bissell is in the Tombs, supra* note 43; affidavit is reprinted in full).

[51] *Id.* at 9 (citing unnamed article in N.Y. WORLD, July 28, 1888); Answer at 31, Bissell v. Press Pub. Co., 17 N.Y.S. 393 (Sup. Ct. 1891).

[52] Complaint, *supra* note 47, at 10 (citing unnamed article in N.Y. WORLD, July 28, 1888).

[53] *Id.* at 15-17 (citing unnamed article in N.Y. WORLD, July 31, 1888).

[54] *Id.* at 17 (citing unnamed article in N.Y. WORLD, Aug. 1, 1888).

[55] *Jared and Champion Still at It*, N.Y. WORLD, Oct. 10, 1888.

[56] *Id.*

[57] Bissell v. Press Pub. Co., 17 N.Y.S. 393, 394 (Sup. Ct. 1891).

[58] *A Batch of Exposures,* N.Y. EVENING WORLD, May 11, 1889, at 9.

[59] CRIMES II, *supra* note 13, at 9.

[60] *Id.* at 9-10.

[61] *Id.* at 13-14.

[62] Advertisement, N.Y. EVENING WORLD, May 9, 1892, at 6. Apparently, Flagg was doing well enough to take a trip to Bermuda during 1892, according to immigration records. Email from Peter Flagg Maxson, *supra* note 15.

[63] Advertisement, N.Y. WORLD, May 7, 1893, at 7.

[64] *New Rental Method*, N.Y. STAR, June 13, 1890, at 4.

[65] CRIMES II, *supra* note 13, at 11-12.

[66] *Id.* at 14.

[67] Unknown, N.Y. HERALD, Feb. 5, 1894, reprinted in 22 FUR TRADE R. 124 (1894).

[68] N.Y. Debt. & Cred. Law § 53.

[69] *Id.*

[70] *Court of Common Pleas, County of New-York*, N.Y. TIMES, March 9, 1894, at 12.

[71] *Jared Flagg's Assets*, N.Y. SUN, April 17, 1894, at 9.

[72] CRIMES II, *supra* note 13, at 12.

[73] *Id.* at 12-13.

[74] *Id.* at 15.

[75] *Id.* at 16-17.

[76] BURROWS & WALLACE, *supra* note 22, at 1186.

Notes to Chapter 2

[1] *Jefferson Market Courthouse*, NewYorkitecture, https://www.newyorkitecture.com/jefferson-market-courthouse/. Once voted the fifth most beautiful buildings in the United States, the building now houses a branch of the New York Public Library. Greenwich Village Society for Historic Preservation, *The Jefferson Market Library*, Off the Grid, https://gvshp.org/blog/2012/02/01/the-jefferson-market-library-a-striking-landmark-shines-again/.

[2] *Agent Flagg Held Responsible for His Tenants*, N.Y. SUN, May 5, 1894, at 7; *A Real Estate Dealer Accused,* N.Y. TRIBUNE, May 5, 1894, at 10.

[3] *Id.*

[4] *Flagg Pleads Not Guilty*, N.Y. Evening World, June 1, 1894, at 7

[5] JARED FLAGG, JR., FLAGG'S FLATS 17 (1908). *See infra* ch. 8 for more information about this book.

[6] *Id.*

[7] *Id.* at 21.

[8] *See generally* DANIEL CZITROM, NEW YORK EXPOSED: THE GILDED AGE POLICE SCANDAL THAT LAUNCHED THE PROGRESSIVE ERA (2016). Czitrom points out that, not only did Lexow expose the "informal but systematic licensing of 'protected' vice," but also the fact that the police committed or permitted "almost every conceivable crime against the elective franchise" on behalf of Tamany Hall. Indeed, the sole New York City member of the committee, Sen. Jacob Cantor, a Tamany man from the Lower East Side, dissented from the committee report, calling it "grossly partisan." *Id.* at 177-78.

[9] Report of the Special Committee Appointed to Investigate the Police Department of the City of New York, S. Rep. No. 25, at 21 (N.Y. 1895) [hereinafter Lexow Committee Report].

[10] *Id.* at 33. *See also* Rachel Amelia Bernstein, Boarding-House Keepers and Brothel Keepers in New York City 1880-1910 (October 1984) (unpublished Ph.D. thesis, Rutgers University) (on file with author).

[11] Lexow Committee Report at 4838.

[12] FLAGG'S FLATS, *supra* note 5, at 35.

[13] *Jared Flagg, Jr., In Court Again*, N.Y. WORLD, June 11, 1895, at 8.

[14] *See, e.g., Wouldn't Pay $100 a Month*, N.Y. TIMES, Oct. 1, 1894, at 5; *To Trap a Captain*, N.Y. WORLD, Oct. 1, 1894, at 5; *From the Pulpit*, DEMOCRAT AND CHRONICLE (Rochester, N.Y.), Oct. 1, 1894; *Blackmail Charge*, NEWS-HERALD (Hillsboro, Ohio), Oct. 4, 1894, at 3.

[15] *Id.*

[16] *Denied by Captain Donohue*, N.Y. TIMES, Oct. 2, 1894, at 2; *Donohue Says Flagg Lies*, N.Y. SUN, Oct. 2, 1894, at 2.

[17] *See, e.g., Women Held for Trial*, N.Y. EVENING WORLD, Oct. 9, 1894, at 7.

[18] *Jared Flagg, Jr., In Court Again*, N.Y. WORLD, June 11, 1895, at 8.

[19] FLAGG'S FLATS, *supra* note 5, at 37.

[20] *Id.* at 40.

[21] *Id.* at 41-57. *See also* CZITROM, *supra* note 8, at 280.

[22] FLAGG'S FLATS, *supra* note 5, at 56-57.

[23] *Indicted Men Named*, BROOKLYN DAILY EAGLE, March 19, 1895, at 1; *Corrupt Police at the Bar*, N.Y. TRIBUNE, March 20, 1894, at 1-2; CZITROM, *supra* note 8, at 280; FLAGG'S FLATS, *supra* note 5, at 57-58.

[24] *See, e.g., Raided by the Police*, BROOKLYN DAILY EAGLE, March 26, 1895, at 1.

[25] *Jared Flagg, Jr., In Court Again*, N.Y. WORLD, June 11, 1895, at 8.

[26] *Id.*

[27] *Jared Flagg, Jr., Anxious to be Tried*, N.Y. TIMES, June 15, 1895, at 9; *Jared Flagg, Jr., Up Again*, N.Y. EVENING WORLD, June 12, 1895, at 3.

[28] *Jared Flagg Indicted*, BROOKLYN DAILY EAGLE, June 21, 1895, at 12.

[29] *Colonel Fellows Moves the Dismissal of Other Indictments*, BROOKLYN DAILY EAGLE, June 17, 1895, at 14.

[30] *Indicted Men May Go Free*, BROOKLYN DAILY EAGLE, Oct.28, 1895 at 4. The Court of Oyer and Terminer was an early criminal court dating back to 1788; it was abolished by the state constitution of 1895 and its jurisdiction transferred to the New York Supreme Court. Historical Society of the New York Courts, https://www.nycourts.gov/history/legal-history-new-york/legal-history-eras-01/history-era-01-court-oyer-terminer.html.

[31] *Police Indictments Dismissed*, N.Y. TIMES, Oct. 30, 1895, at 14.

[32] *Capt. Strauss Bounced*, N.Y. SUN, Nov. 23, 1895, at 2.

[33] *Police Indictments Quashed*, BROOKLYN DAILY EAGLE, Dec. 26, 1895, at 14.

[34] *Police Officers Commended*, N.Y. TRIBUNE, Aug. 10, 1895, at 10.

[35] *Trial of Jared Flagg*, N.Y. TIMES, Feb. 27, 1896, at 7.

[36] *Jared Flagg, Jr., Again Arrested*, NEW HAVEN DAILY MORNING JOURNAL & COURIER, Sept. 11, 1895, at 3.

[37] *Jared Flagg, Jr., Lays All His Troubles at Dr. J.A.B. Wilson's Door*, N.Y. TRIBUNE, Sept. 18, 1895, at 11; *Flagg Blames Dr. J.A.B. Wilson*, N.Y. TIMES, Sept. 18, 1895, at 15.

[38] *Court of General Sessions*, N.Y. TIMES, Oct. 29, 1895, at 14.

[39] *Pastor Wilson's Testimony*, S.F. CALL, Nov. 10, 1895, at 2.

[40] *Dr. Wilson as Joseph*, DELAWARE GAZETTE & STATE JOURNAL, Nov. 21, 1895, at 2.

[41] *Id.*

[42] *Trial of Jared Flagg, Jr.*, N.Y. TIMES, Feb. 21, 1896, at 14.

[43] *Id.*

[44] *Stories of Flagg's Flats*, N.Y. SUN, Feb. 22, 1896, at 9.

[45] *Id.*

[46] FLAGG'S FLATS, *supra* note 5, at 62-63.

[47] *Trial of Jared Flagg*, N.Y. TIMES , Feb. 27, 1896, at 7.

[48] *Jared Flagg A Broker Now*, N.Y. SUN, April 6, 1907, at 5.

[49] *Verdict Against Flagg*, N.Y. TIMES, Feb. 28, 1896, at 3.

[50] *Judge Newburger Requires No Advice*, N.Y. DAILY TRIBUNE, March 24, 1896, at 5.

[51] People v. Flagg, 42 N.Y.S. 1130 (App. Div. 1896).

[52] FLAGG'S FLATS, *supra* note 5, at 103.

[53] People v. Flagg, 12 A.D. 628 (1896).

[54] *Flagg, Jr., in the Tombs*, N.Y. TIMES, Dec. 23, 1896, at 9; *Flagg, Jr., in the Tombs*, N.Y. SUN, Dec. 23, 1896. Both of these articles erroneously stated that Flagg had been convicted of renting flats for purposes of prostitution.

[55] *City and Vicinity*, N.Y. TIMES, Dec. 27, 1896, at 3 (writ of certiorari issued); *Jared Flagg, Jr., Still in the Tombs*, N.Y. SUN, Dec. 31, at 8 (habeas corpus petition argued).

[56] *Flagg's Tenants Put on Oath*, N.Y. SUN, Nov. 29, 1896, at 3.

[57] FLAGG'S FLATS, *supra* note 5, at 116.

[58] *Id.* at 97. *See also Jared Flagg A Broker Now*, N.Y. SUN, April 6, 1907, at 5.

Notes to Chapter 3

[1] JARED FLAGG, JR., FLAGG'S FLATS 116 (1910).

[2] *Id.* at 117–118.

[3] *Id.* at 120 (emphasis in the original).

[4] *Id.* at 120–121.

[5] *Id.* at 124.

[6] *Id.*

[7] *Help Wanted—Females*, N.Y. SUN, Feb. 12, 1903, 11.

[8] *Help Wanted—Females*, N.Y. SUN, Feb. 22, 1903, 8.

[9] *Help Wanted—Females*, N.Y. TIMES, Nov. 17, 1904, 16.

[10] FLAGG'S FLATS, *supra* note 1, at 124.

[11] *Id.*

[12] *Id.* at 125.

[13] *Id.* at 126–134.

[14] *Id.* at 134–138.

[15] *See, e.g., Posed, But Unpaid, She Says*, N.Y. SUN, Feb. 18, 1904 (model who claimed she posed for photographs, but was not paid her $12 fee, asked court clerk to send any money recovered to Flagg and identified Flagg as her agent).

[16] FLAGG'S FLATS, *supra* note 1, at 139.

[17] *Id.* at 141–146.

[18] *Id.*

[19] *Id.* at 147–153.

[20] N.Y. SUN, Sept. 24, 1904, at 4.

[21] *Id.*

[22] *The Flagg Conviction*, N.Y. SUN, Sept. 27, 1904, at 12.

[23] *Id.*

[24] FLAGG'S FLATS, *supra* note 1, at 154.

[25] *Id.* at 151-165.

[26] *Id.* at 165.

[27] *To Improve Employment Agencies*, N.Y. TRIBUNE, Jan. 7, 1905, at 5; *Speakers Urge Actors To Unionize the Stage*, N.Y. TIMES, Jan. 14, 1905, at 9.

[28] *See, e.g., Big Rush for "Panama" Jobs*, N.Y. SUN, Jan. 12, 1905, at 5 (describes fraudulent employment agencies offering white collar jobs such as bookkeepers, clerks, and timekeepers with the Panama Canal Commission, when no such jobs existed except through the civil service); *School Men Held*, N.Y. TIMES, Jan. 12, 1905 (describing the arrest and court appearance of three men involved in the Panama Canal scam).

[29] *Speakers Urge Actors To Unionize the Stage*, N.Y. TIMES, Jan. 14, 1905, at 9.

[30] *Id.* The term "hat book" seems to have disappeared from the lexicon; presumably, Keating was referring to agents who kept their book of clients in their hats, i.e., fly-by-night operators.

[31] *To Arrest Theatre Men*, N.Y. TRIBUNE, Jan. 14, 1905, at 9.

[32] FLAGG'S FLATS, *supra* note 1, at 165.

[33] *See, e.g., Revoked Employment Agency License*, N.Y. TIMES, Jan. 24, 1905, at 9 (agency charged as an "adjunct of the 'cadet' system," that is, steering young women, often immigrants, applying for work into prostitution through pimps known as "cadets"); *Aid Keating in Fight for Girls*, N.Y. EVENING WORLD, Jan. 24, 1905, at 9 (citing numerous incidents that prompted license revocation); *Fight Over Victims*, N.Y. TRIBUNE, Jan. 25, 1905 (describing competition among cadets for attractive women); *Commissioner Keating's Work*, N.Y. TRIBUNE, Jan. 27, 1905 (reporting revocation of license of employment agency charged with operating for immoral purposes); *Evil Employment Agencies*, N.Y. SUN, Jan. 29, 1905 (discussing at length the way employment agencies were used to direct immigrant women into brothels).

[34] *School Men Held*, N.Y. TIMES, Jan. 13, 1905.

[35] FLAGG'S FLATS, *supra* note 1, at 171.

[36] *Id.* at 175-177.

[37] *Id.* at 180-181.

[38] *Id.* at 177-178.

[39] *Id.* at 173.

[40] *Id.* at 182-187.

[41] *Women Attack Jared Flagg*, N.Y. SUN, April 29, 1906, at 14.

[42] FLAGG'S FLATS, *supra* note 1, at 196-200. Charlotte Odlum Smith (1940-1917) was hardly that; she was indeed the founder of the Woman's Rescue League and a highly regard advocate for women's rights. Kristin Holt, *Charlotte Smith Demands National Legislation to Require Matrimony,* http://www.kristinholt. com/archives/4026; *Charlotte Smith: A Groundbreaking Advocate for Women's Rights*, ADIRONDACK ALMANACK, July 2, 2012, https://www.adirondackalmanack.com/2012/07/charlotte-smith-groundbreaking-advocate-for-womens-rights.html.

[43] *Women Attack Jared Flagg*, N.Y. SUN, April 29, 1906, at 14.

[44] *No License for Flagg*, N.Y. TIMES, May 3, 1906, at 16.

[45] *Flagg Against License Bureau*, N.Y. TRIBUNE, Sept. 23, 1906.

[46] FLAGG'S FLATS, *supra* note 1, at 259-262.

[47] *Id.* at 267-273.

[48] *Id.* at 275.

[49] *Id.* at 279. *See also Jared Flagg A Broker Now*, N.Y. SUN, April 6, 1907, at 5.

[50] FLAGG'S FLATS, *supra* note 1, at 224-225.

[51] *Help Wanted—Females*, N.Y. Times, Nov. 17, 1904, at 16.

[52] FLAGG'S FLATS, *supra* note 1, at 229 (citing N.Y. MORNING TELEGRAPH, May 2, 1906, and including a letter from Auburn State Prison Warden George W. Benham certifying that Flagg was never there).

[53] FLAGG'S FLATS, *supra* note 1, at 230 (citing N.Y. WORLD, May 3, 1906).

[54] FLAGG'S FLATS, *supra* note 1, at 259.

Notes to Chapter 4

[1] *See, e.g., Flagg's New Graft 'Has Millions In It,'* N.Y. TIMES, April 6, 1907, at 16; *Jared Flagg a Broker Now,* N.Y. SUN, April 6, 1907, at 5.

[2] *Flagg's New Graft 'Has Millions In It,'* N.Y. TIMES, April 6, 1907, at 16.

[3] JARED FLAGG, THE FLAGG RAID 6 (1912) [hereinafter RAID]. This small book, part of the Cornell University Library Digital Collections, claims to have had three printings in 1912: Jan. 26—2,000, Feb. 8—10,000, and March 12—50,000. In 1920, essentially the same story, with some variations in language and a new, much happier ending, would be published as Part II of THE CRIMES OF JARED FLAGG (1920) [hereinafter CRIMES II]. *See infra* ch. 8 for more information about these books.

[4] As listed in JOHN FOSTER KIRK, A SUPPLEMENT TO 1 ALLIBONE'S CRITICAL DICTIONARY OF ENGLISH LITERATURE AND BRITISH AND AMERICAN AUTHORS 600 (1899).

[5] Richard D. Wyckoff, *Looking Forward—and Backward After Thirty-Five Years in Wall Street,* 33 MAG. OF WALL ST. 298, 301 (No. 4, Dec. 22, 1923).

[6] RAID, *supra* note 3, at 8-9. Flagg notes that this is sometimes called the "Pettibone Progressive System."

[7] *Jared Flagg a Broker Now,* N.Y. SUN, April 6, 1907, at 5.

[8] *Id.*

[9] *Trading on a Scale: Is There a Safe Method of Operating on This Plan?,* 5 TICKER & INV. DIG. 170 (No. 4, February 1910).

[10] CRIMES II, *supra* note 3, at 158.

[11] Brief on Behalf of the United States, April 6, 1916, United States v. Flagg, 233 F. 481 (2d Cir. 1916) (No. 196), on file at National Archives & Records Administration, Kansas City, Mo., Case File No. 5619, at 10.

[12] *Business Opportunities,* DEMOCRAT AND CHRONICLE (Rochester, N.Y.), Jan. 12, 1908, at 3.

[13] *Business Opportunities,* DAILY JOURNAL (Meriden, Conn.), Feb. 5, 1908, at 11.

[14] CRIMES II, *supra* note 3, at 158-59.

[15] Brief on Behalf of the United States, April 6, 1916, United States v. Flagg, 233 F. 481 (2d Cir. 1916) (No. 196), on file at National Archives & Records Administration, Kansas City, Mo., Case File No. 5619, at 10.

[16] MIKE WALLACE, GREATER GOTHAM, A HISTORY OF NEW YORK FROM 1898 TO 1919, at 95-96 (2017) [hereinafter GREATER GOTHAM]; Yale M. Braunstein, *The*

Role of Information Failures in the Financial Meltdown (2009) (PowerPoint presentation at https://web.archive.org/web/20091222041754/ http://people.ischool.berkeley.edu/~bigyale/fin_meltdown/InformationFailures_ 080409_color. ppt, slide 34.

[17] *Jared Flagg a Broker Now*, N.Y. EVENING SUN, April 6, 1907, at 5.

[18] *Flagg Bunch in Jail All Day*, N.Y. SUN, Sept. 25, 1911, at 1.

[19] RAID, *supra* note 3, at 13.

[20] CRIMES II, *supra* note 3, at 160.

[21] *Rapid-Wealth Plan Exhibits Hand of Flagg*, N.Y. EVENING WORLD, Aug. 26, 1908, at 11.

[22] CRIMES II, *supra* note 3, at 159-60.

[23] *Id.* at 161

[24] *Personal and Pertinent*, TIMES-TRIBUNE (Scranton, Pa.), Oct. 17, 1910, at 6. This article, and others like it, were apparently drawn from an article in the NEW YORK AMERICAN.

[25] According to one Flagg family historian, "[We] in the family are eternally grateful to Mr. Ponzi, so that, say, Bernard Madoff was not accused of running a Flagg Scheme! … We Flaggs strive for excellence in our chosen fields, and surely Uncle Jared excelled at his!" Email from Peter Flagg Maxson, June 2020, on file with author.

[26] RAID, *supra* note 3, at 54-55.

[27] *Investors in Flagg Scheme Here Alarmed*, Bridgeport (Conn.) TIMES AND EVENING FARMER, Oct. 19, 1910, at 10.

[28] *Postal Inspectors Raid Jared Flagg*, N.Y. TIMES, Sept. 24, 1911, at 1.

[29] CRIMES II, *supra* note 3, at 163.

[30] RAID, *supra* note 3, at 55-56.

[31] *Ex-U.S. Treasurer Arrested in Raid*, N.Y. TRIBUNE, Sept. 24, 1911, at 1.

[32] *Id.*; *Pinch Flagg's 52 Percenters*, N.Y. SUN, Sept. 24, 1911, p. 1; *Postal Inspectors Raid Jared Flagg*, N.Y. TIMES, Sept. 24, 1911, at 1.

[33] *Ex-U.S. Treasurer Arrested in Raid*, N.Y. TRIBUNE, Sept. 24, 1911, at 1.

[34] *Former U.S. Treasurer Is Lodged in the Tombs*, BROOKLYN DAILY EAGLE, Sept. 24, 1911, at 6.

[35] *See* RAID, *supra* note 3, at 32.

[36] *Id.* at 51.

[37] CRIMES II, *supra* note 3, at 163.

[38] RAID, *supra* note 3, at 17-23.

[39] *Id.*

[40] *Ex-U.S. Treasurer Arrested in Raid*, N.Y. TRIBUNE, Sept. 24, 1911, at 1.

[41] *Id.*; RAID, *supra* note 3, at 20.

[42] *See, e.g., Postal Inspectors Raid Jared Flagg*, N.Y. TIMES, Sept. 24, 1911, at 1; *Ex-U.S. Treasurer Arrested in Raid*, N.Y. TRIBUNE, Sept. 24, 1911, at 1; *Pinch Flagg's 52 Percenters*, N.Y. SUN, Sept. 24, 1911, at 1; *Former U.S. Treasurer Is Lodged in the Tombs*, BROOKLYN DAILY EAGLE, Sept. 24, 1911, at 6; *Eight are Charged with Violation of Postal Laws*, BUFFALO COURIER, Sept. 24, 1911, at 33; *Prominent Men Taken in Raid on Broker's Office*, BUFFALO TIMES, Sept. 24, 1911, at 21; *Federal Raid Nets Ex-U.S. Treasurer and Clergyman*, BUFFALO SUNDAY MORNING NEWS, Sept. 24, 1911, at 25.

[43] *Many Protesting Customers Taken to Court in Taxicabs as Witnesses*, N.Y. SUN, Sept. .24, 1911, at 1.

[44] *Ex-U.S. Treasurer Arrested in Raid*, N.Y. TRIBUNE, Sept. 24, 1911, at 1. The reference is to a notorious con artist nicknamed "520 Percent Miller" who, in 1899, promised 10% return on investment each week. *See William Miller, the Original Schemer*, TIME, March 7, 2012.

[45] A scam in which one F. Ewart Storey purported to pay 2½ to 3 per cent a month from speculation in cotton, but seems never to have purchased a single bale. *Storey Cotton Co.*, 15 UNITED STATES INVESTOR 1398 (No. 38, Sept. 17, 1904), https://www.google.com/books/edition/United_States_Investor/CZg4hYFbOy8 C?hl=en&gbpv=1&dq=storey+cotton+operations&pg=PA1398&printsec=frontc over.

[46] *Ex-U.S. Treasurer Arrested in Raid*, N.Y. TRIBUNE, Sept. 24, 1911, at 1.

[47] *Pinch Flagg's 52 Percenters*, N.Y. SUN, Sept. 24, 1911, at 1.

[48] *Eight are Charged with Violation of Postal Laws*, BUFFALO COURIER, Sept. 24, 1911, at 33.

[49] CRIMES II, *supra* note 3, at 163-64.

[50] *Brothers to Aid Flagg*, N.Y. TRIBUNE, Sept. 25, 1911, at 4.

[51] *Id.*

[52] *Eight Are Charged with Violation of Postal Laws*, BUFFALO (N.Y.) COURIER, Sept. 24, 1911, at 33.

[53] *Flagg Gives $25,000 Bail, Hustles to Free Others in Get-Rich-Quick Case*, N.Y. EVENING WORLD, Sept. 25, 1911, at 16.

[54] *Id.*

[55] *Brothers to Aid Flagg*, N.Y. TRIBUNE, Sept. 25, 1911, at 4.

[56] *Jared Flagg Bailed; Brother Puts Up Realty*, BROOKLYN DAILY EAGLE, Sept. 25, 1911, at 2. These properties apparently comprised Ernest Flagg's home and studio, both of which he designed. Email from Peter Flagg Maxson, *supra* note 25.

[57] *Flagg and Friends Out*, N.Y. TRIBUNE, Sept. 26, 1911, at 12.

[58] Flagg would later say Russe was a "ten-dollar-a-week telephone clerk," with orders to "instruct my fourteen brokers" when to buy or sell stocks. *Flagg, Free, Says He's Persecuted*, N.Y. TIMES, Sept. 26, 1911, at 7. Russe is a mysterious figure who shows up at various times in Flagg's story. For some particularly sultry photographs, see *Madeline Russe*, BUFFALO (N.Y.) ENQUIRER, Sept. 27, 1911, at 1; *New Picture of Madeline Russe*, BUFFALO (N.Y.) ENQUIRER, Sept. 29, 1911, at 9; and *Caught At Last! A Wolf Who Has Preyed on Innocent Girls for 25 Years*, GREENSBORO (N.C.) DAILY NEWS, Nov. 22, 1914, at 2. *See infra* ch. 5, text accompanying note 3.

[59] *Cashier of Flagg's Company Arrested*, BUFFALO (N.Y.) COURIER, Sept. 26, 1911, at 1.

[60] *Flagg Gives $25,000 Bail, Hustles to Free Others in Get-Rich-Quick Case*, N.Y. EVENING WORLD, Sept. 25, 1911, at 16; *Flagg Gets Order to Show Cause*, BUFFALO (N.Y.) ENQUIRER, Sept. 16, 1911, at 1.

[61] *Flagg Gives $25,000 Bail, Hustles to Free Others in Get-Rich-Quick Case*, N.Y. EVENING WORLD, Sept. 25, 1911, at 16.

[62] *Cashier of Flagg's Company Arrested*, BUFFALO (N.Y.) COURIER, Sept. 26, 1911, at 1.

[63] *Flagg and Friends Out*, N.Y. TRIBUNE, Sept. 26, 1911, at 12; *Flagg, Free, Says He's Persecuted*, N.Y. TIMES, Sept. 26, 1911, at 7.

[64] *Flagg, Free, Says He's Persecuted*, N.Y. TIMES, Sept. 26, 1911, at 7.

[65] Affidavit and Order to Show Cause (Sept. 26, 1911), Transcript of Record at 87, United States v. Flagg, 233 F. 481 (2d Cir. 1916) (No. 196), on file at National Archives & Records Administration, Kansas City, Mo., Case File No. 5619. *See also Flagg Gets Order to Show Cause*, BUFFALO (N.Y.) ENQUIRER, Sept. 26, 1911, at 1; *Flagg Sues for His Books*, BROOKLYN DAILY EAGLE, Sept. 26, 1911, at 1.

[66] *Grand Jury May Act To-Day in Flagg Case*, N.Y. TIMES, Sept. 27, 1911, at 22.

Notes to Chapter 5

[1] *Flagg is Indicted with His Associates*, N.Y. TIMES, Sept. 28, 1911, at 4.

[2] *Neely Fails to Get Bail*, N.Y. TIMES, Sept. 29, 1911, at 4.

[3] *Madeline Russe Turns Up*, N.Y. TIMES, Sept. 29, 1911, at 22.

[4] *Woman's Quarrel Brought Flagg into Lime Light*, BUFFALO (N.Y.) TIMES, Sept. 28, 1911, at 1.

[5] *Hazel Murray, Show-Girl Protégé of Flagg*, DEMOCRAT & CHRONICLE (Rochester, N.Y.), Sept. 29, 2911, at 1.

[6] *Flagg Defended by His Brother*, DEMOCRAT & CHRONICLE (Rochester, N.Y.), Sept. 27, 2911, at 1.

[7] JARED FLAGG, THE FLAGG RAID 98 (1912) [hereinafter RAID].

[8] *Flagg is Indicted with His Associates*, N.Y. TIMES, Sept. 28, 1911, at 4.

[9] *Madeline Russe Turns Up*, N.Y. TIMES, Sept. 29, 1911, at 22.

[10] *Harris Took Flyer on Flagg's Stocks*, BUFFALO (N.Y.) ENQUIRER, Sept. 27, 1911, at 7.

[11] *Flagg Customer Put In $220,000*, N.Y. TIMES, Oct. 1, 1911, at 18.

[12] *They Like Flagg Dividends*, N.Y. SUN, Oct. 1, 1911, at 3.

[13] *Have Confidence in Flagg*, N.Y. TRIBUNE, Oct. 3, 1911, at 2.

[14] Brief for Plaintiff-in-Error at 38, United States v. Flagg, 233 F. 481 (2d Cir. 1916) (No. 196), on file at National Archives & Records Administration, Kansas City, Mo., Case File No. 5619.

[15] *Winding Up Flagg's Pool*, N.Y. TIMES, Oct. 26, 1911, at 10.

[16] A symbol of cowardice during World War I. *See Nicoletta F. Gullace*, 36 J. BRITISH STUD. 178 (1997)

[17] *Winding Up Flagg's Pool*, N.Y. TIMES, Oct. 26, 1911, at 10.

[18] JARED FLAGG, THE CRIMES OF JARED FLAGG 176 (1920) [hereinafter CRIMES II].

[19] Ernest Flagg, Diaries, on file at the Architectural and Fine Arts Library at Columbia University.

[20] *Girl Sues Federal Officer*, N.Y. TIMES, Feb. 7, 1912, at 1; *Lawyer Violent, Girl Asks $1,000*, N.Y. EVENING WORLD, Feb. 7, 1912, at 4.

[21] Indictment of July 17th, 1912, 1 Transcript of Record at 6, United States v. Flagg, 233 F. 481 (2d Cir. 1916) (No. 196), on file at National Archives & Records Administration, Kansas City, Mo., Case File No. 5619 [hereinafter Indictment].

[22] *Id.* at 6-19.

[23] *Id.* at 21.

[24] *Id.* at 38-61.

[25] *Id.* at 19.

[26] *Id.* at 20.

[27] *Id.* at 22.

[28] *Id.* at 23.

[29] *Id.* at 38-61.

[30] *Id.*

[31] *Jared Flagg in Court*, N.Y. SUN, July 19, 1912, at 13.

[32] *James Shock (sic) is Dead*, N.Y. TRIBUNE, Aug. 11, 1912, at 9.

[33] *Jared Flagg in Court Again*, N.Y. SUN, Dec. 3, 1912, at 2.

[34] *Only a Trial Can Prove Facts in the Case*, BUFFALO (N.Y.) COMMERCIAL, Feb. 4, 1913, at 2.

[35] *Jared Flagg to be Tried*, N.Y. EVENING WORLD, Feb. 17, 1913, at 12.

[36] One item in the TIMES noted that Flagg had satisfied a judgment against him on May 6, 1913, for $182 in favor of E. R. Carroll et al. *Judgments Satisfied*, N.Y. TIMES, June 5, 1913, at 14.

[37] Crimes II, *supra* note 14, at 178.

[38] *Jared Flagg to be His Own Lawyer at Trial*, N.Y. SUN, Oct. 20, 1914, at 16. *See also Jared Flagg Trial Begun*, WALL ST. J., Oct. 20, 1914, at 6; *Flagg Trial To-Day After Three Years*, N.Y. SUN, Oct. 19, 1914, at 8; *Jared Flagg Trial Opens*, DEMOCRAT & CHRONICLE (Rochester, N.Y.), Oct. 20, 1914, at 3; *Broker to Defend Self*, N.Y. TRIBUNE, Oct. 20, 1914, at 6.

[39] Judge Rudkin was formally assigned to the Eastern District of Washington. Federal Judicial Center, U.S. District Court for the District of Washington: Judges, https://www.fjc.gov/history/courts/u.s.-district-court-eastern-district-washington-judges

[40] *Id.*

[41] *Seven Jurors Challenged in Trial of Jared Flagg*, BUFFALO (N.Y.) COURIER, Oct. 21, 1914, at 1.

[42] *Flagg Scores in Mail Fraud Suit*, N.Y. TRIBUNE, Oct. 21, 1914, at 9.

[43] Bill of Exceptions, Transcript of Record at 93, United States v. Flagg, 233 F. 481 (2d Cir. 1916) (No. 196), on file at National Archives & Records Administration, Kansas City, Mo., Case File No. 5619 [hereinafter Exceptions].

[44] *Id.* at 95.

[45] United States v. Weeks, 232 U.S. 383, 398 (1914).

[46] Exceptions, *supra* note 43, at 96.

[47] Ex parte Flagg, 236 U.S. 683 (1914).

[48] Exceptions, *supra* note 43, at 98.

[49] *Flagg Scores in Mail Fraud Suit*, N.Y. TRIBUNE, Oct. 21, 1914, at 9.

[50] *Flagg's Rights Were Invaded*, POUGHKEEPSIE (N.Y.) EAGLE-NEWS, Oct. 23, 1914, at 1.

[51] Exceptions, *supra* note 43, at 98-101.

[52] *Ignorant of Wash Sales*, N,Y. TRIBUNE, Oct. 22, 1914, at 12.

[53] *Jurors Laugh at Quips of Flagg*, N.Y. TRIBUNE, Oct. 23, 1914, at 12; *Jared Flagg Lucky as His Own Lawyer*, N.Y. SUN, Oct. 23, 1914, at 6.

[54] Ex parte Flagg, 236 U.S. 683 (1914).

[55] *Jared Flagg's Stock Business*, WALL ST. J., Oct. 27, 1914, at 2.

[56] RAID *supra* note 7, at 41 (1912).

[57] Exceptions, *supra* note 43, at 225-27.

[58] *Id.* at 228-31.

[59] *Id.* at 236.

[60] *Id.* at 243.

[61] *Id.* at 249-50.

[62] *Id.* at 253.

[63] *Id.* at 267.

[64] *Id.* at 276.

[65] *Novel Move Made for Flagg*, N.Y. SUN, Oct. 29, 1914, at 7.

[66] Exceptions, *supra* note 43, at 389.

[67] *Id.* at 389-391.

[68] *Id.* at 391-395.

[69] *Id.* at 395.

[70] *Id.*

[71] *Id.* at 404.

[72] *Id.* at 424.

[73] *Swears Flagg Paid $600,000 to Clients*, ITHACA (N.Y.) JOURNAL, Oct. 30 1914, at 1.

[74] Exceptions, *supra* note 43, at 498.

[75] *Id.* at 500-511. *See also Attorney for Indicted Broker to Sum Up Monday*, DEMOCRAT & CHRONICLE (Rochester, N.Y.), Oct. 31, 1914, at 3.

[76] Exceptions, *supra* note 43, at 512-13.

[77] CRIMES II, *supra* note 18, at 181.

[78] Exceptions, *supra* note 43, at 514.

[79] *Flagg Convicted of Stock Frauds,* N.Y. TIMES, Nov. 3, 1914, at 18.

[80] CRIMES II, *supra* note 18, at 182.

[81] Exceptions, *supra* note 43, at 517.

[82] *Id.* at 524-25.

[83] *Flagg Convicted of Stock Frauds,* N.Y. TIMES, Nov. 3, 1914, at 18.

[84] *Id.* at 528.

[85] *Flagg Guilty Fraud Charged*, STAR-GAZETTE (Elmira, N.Y.), Nov. 3, 1914, at 2.

[86] *Arrested Careers*, N.Y. EVENING WORLD, Nov. 4, 1914, at 16.

[87] CRIMES II, *supra* note 18, at 183.

[88] *Flagg Guilty Fraud Charged*, STAR-GAZETTE (Elmira, N.Y.), Nov. 3, 1914, at 2.

[89] *Jared Flagg Guilty of $1,500,000 Fraud*, N.Y. SUN, Nov. 3, 1914, at 6.

[90] CRIMES II, *supra* note 18, at 183.

[91] *Id.* at 184.

Notes to Chapter 6

[1] Motion to Arrest and Vacate Judgment of Conviction and to Set Aside Verdict, Nov. 6, 1914, in Bill of Exceptions, Transcript of Record at 529, United States v. Flagg, 233 F. 481 (2d Cir. 1916) (No. 196), on file at National Archives & Records Administration, Kansas City, Mo., Case File No. 5619 [hereinafter Exceptions].

[2] *Flagg Pleads Hard to Avoid Sentence*, N.Y. TIMES, Nov. 7, 1914, at 7.

[3] *Id.*

[4] *Flagg Gets Adjournment*, BROOKLYN DAILY EAGLE, Nov. 10, 1914, at 3.

[5] Motion to Arrest and Vacate Judgment of Conviction and to Set Aside Verdict, Nov. 6, 1914, in Exceptions, *supra* note 1, at 534-35.

[6] Supplemental Motion to Arrest and Vacate Judgment of Conviction and to Set Aside Verdict, Nov. 17, 1914, in Exceptions, *supra* note 1, at 536-545.

[7] Judgment of the Court, Nov. 17, 1914, in Exceptions, *supra* note 1, at 545. *See also Flagg Gets 18 Months*, N.Y. TIMES, Nov. 18, 1914, at 5.

[8] *Flagg's Partners Free*, Buffalo (N.Y.) Morning Express, Nov. 18, 1914, at 8. The fact that Flagg had been acquitted on the single charge of conspiracy surely also influenced Marshall's decision.

[9] *52% Flagg* (advertisement), BEAVER FALLS (PA.) TRIBUNE, Jan. 9, 1915, at 8.

[10] Bill of Complaint, in Transcript of Record, Cook v. Flagg, 233 F. 426 (2d Cir. 1916) (No. 297), on file at National Archives & Records Administration, Kansas City, Mo., Case File No. 6205, at 14 [hereinafter Transcript]. *See infra* Chapter 7.

[11] Order (extending filing deadline to May 15, 1915), filed April 22, 1915, and Order (extending filing deadline for exhibits to Sept. 30, 1915), filed Nov. 2, 1915, United States v. Flagg, 233 F. 481 (2d Cir. 1916) (No. 196), on file at National Archives & Records Administration, Kansas City, Mo., Case File No. 5619.

[12] Deposition of Owen N. Brown, Feb. 9, 1916, at 1, in Affidavits and Notice of Motion, United States v. Flagg, 233 F. 481 (2d Cir. 1916) (No. 196), on file at National Archives & Records Administration, Kansas City, Mo., Case File No. 5619 [hereinafter Affidavits].

[13] *Id.*

[14] Transcript of Telegram from Littleton to Rudkin, Jan. 25, 1916, in Affidavits, *supra* note 12, at Exhibit A.

[15] Letter from Littleton to Rudkin, Jan. 25, 1916, in Affidavits, *supra* note 12, at Exhibit B.

[16] Correspondence between Littleton and Rudkin, Jan. 25, 26, 31 & Feb. 1, in Affidavits, *supra* note 12, at Exhibit C, D, E & F.

[17] Petition for Writ of Certiorari, Feb. 14, 1916, in Affidavits, *supra* note 12, at 1.

[18] Stipulation Re Amendment of Transcript of Record, Feb. 14, 1916, United States v. Flagg, 233 F. 481 (2d Cir. 1916) (No. 196), on file at National Archives & Records Administration, Kansas City, Mo., Case File No. 5619.

[19] Brief for Plaintiff-in-Error, Feb. 5, 1916, United States v. Flagg, 233 F. 481 (2d Cir. 1916) (No. 196), on file at National Archives & Records Administration, Kansas City, Mo., Case File No. 5619, at 37-73.

[20] *Id.* at 73-124.

[21] Id. at 124-25.

[22] *Id.* at 125.

[23] Brief on Behalf of the United States, April 6, 1916, United States v. Flagg, 233 F. 481 (2d Cir. 1916) (No. 196), on file at National Archives & Records Administration, Kansas City, Mo., Case File No. 5619, at 42 [hereinafter Brief for United States].

[24] *Id.* at 43.

[25] *Id.* at 44.

[26] *Id.* at 45.

[27] *Id.* at 49.

[28] Boyd v. United States, 116 U.S. 616.

[29] Brief for the United States, *supra* note 23, at 52.

[30] *Id.* at 55.

[31] *See* ch. 5, *supra,* note 45 and accompanying text.

[32] Brief for the United States, *supra* note 23, at 68.

[33] *Id.* at 70.

[34] Flagg v. United States, 233 F. 481, 482 (2d Cir. 1916).

[35] *Id.* at 483.

[36] *Id.*

[37] *Id.* at 486.

[38] *Id.* (Veeder, J., concurring). *See also Jared Flagg Freed by Official Errors*, N.Y. TIMES, May 10, 1916, at 9.

³⁹ Order for Mandate, May 19, 1916, United States v. Flagg, 233 F. 481 (2d Cir. 1916) (No. 196), on file at National Archives & Records Administration, Kansas City, Mo., Case File No. 5619.

⁴⁰ *Igel Attorneys Plan To Use Flagg Ruling*, N.Y. TRIBUNE, May 12, 1916, at 4; *Von Igel Will Fight To Get Papers Back*, N.Y. SUN, May 12, 1916, at 5.

⁴¹ JARED FLAGG, THE CRIMES OF JARED FLAGG 186-87 (1920).

⁴² *See* ch. 7, *infra*.

⁴³ *Id.* at 189-90.

⁴⁴ *Id.* at 187-88.

Notes to Chapter 7

¹ Bill of Complaint, in Transcript of Record, Cook v. Flagg, 251 F. 5 (2d Cir. 1918) (No. 297), on file at National Archives & Records Administration, Kansas City, Mo., Case File No. 6205, at 15-16 [hereinafter Transcript]. *See also* E. Ellsworth Cook, Find A Grave, at https://www.findagrave.com/ memorial/ 83323521/e.-ellsworth-cook.

² *Id.* at 26.

³ See generally ERIC B. EASTON, DEFENDING THE MASSES: A PROGRESSIVE LAWYER'S BATTLES FOR FREE SPEECH (2018).

⁴ Bill of Complaint, in Transcript, *supra* note 1, at 14-15.

⁵ JARED FLAGG, THE CRIMES OF JARED FLAGG 339 (1920) [hereinafter CRIMES I]. Most of the printed versions Flagg's book available today, including the one referenced in ch. 1-6, do not mention the civil case; as will be explained more fully in ch. 8, these are called CRIMES II herein. The civil case appears only in a longer, presumably earlier version, called CRIMES I, and available at the Internet Archive at http://archive.org/stream/crimesofjared00flag?ref=ol#page/ n1/mode/ 2up.

⁶ Defendant's Answer, in Transcript, *supra* note 1, at 45-58.

⁷ *Id.*

⁸ Cook v. Flagg, 255 F. 195, 196 (S.D.N.Y. 1915). *See* ch. 5, *supra,* text accompanying note 34.

⁹ Philipp v. S.S. McClure, *aff'd*, S.S. McClure v. Philipp, 170 F. 910 (2d Cir. 1909).

¹⁰ *Cook*, 255 F. at 196.

¹¹ *Id.* at 198-99.

[12] *Receiver for Jared Flagg*, N.Y. TIMES, Sept. 28, 2915, at 5.

[13] *Creditors Seeking Jared Flagg's Cash*, N.Y. SUN, Oct. 7, 1915, at 5.

[14] Bill of Complaint, in Transcript, *supra* note 1, at 24.

[15] *Hail Flaggs to Court*, N.Y. TIMES, Oct. 7, 1915, at 20.

[16] *Id. See also Creditors Seeking Jared Flagg's Cash*, N.Y. SUN, Oct. 7, 1915, at 5.

[17] Trial Transcript, in Transcript, *supra* note 1, at 72.

[18] *Id.* at 73-78.

[19] *Id.* at 79-81.

[20] *Id.* at 82.

[21] *Id.* at 95-96.

[22] *Id.* at 558-59.

[23] *Id.* at 948-63.

[24] Cook v. Flagg, 233 F.426 (2d Cir. 1916).

[25] *Id.* at 427-28.

[26] Cook v. Flagg, 233 F. 713 (S.D.N.Y. 1916).

[27] *Jared Flagg Lecture* (advertisement), WALL ST. J., Dec. 2 & 5, 1916; N.Y. EVE. WORLD, Dec. 6, 1916.

[28] *Flagg Gives Secret of Beating Wall St.,* N.Y. SUN, Dec. 5, 1916, at 5.

[29] Decree, in Transcript, *supra* note 1, at 1531.

[30] CRIMES I, *supra* note 5, at 340-44.

[31] Opinion of Judge A. N. Hand (S.D.N.Y), May 1, 1917, on file at National Archives & Records Administration, Kansas City, Mo., Case File No. 6205. *See, also Receiver for Flagg*, POST-STAR (Glens Falls, N.Y.), May 2, 1917, at 7; *Fraudulent Stock Dealings*, ONEONTA (N.Y.) STAR, May 2, 1917, at 1; *Victims Share in Big Swindle of Jared Flagg*, STAR-GAZETTE (Elmira, N.Y.), May 4, 1917, at 10; *Flagg Creditors May Get Some Money Back*, ITHACA (N.Y.) J., May 7, 1917, at 6.

[31] *Receivers' Notice* (advertisement), N.Y. TIMES, May 19, 1917, at 16.

[32] Opinion of Judge A. N. Hand (S.D.N.Y), May 1, 1917, on file at National Archives & Records Administration, Kansas City, Mo., Case File No. 6205, at 7-8.

[33] Decree, in Transcript, *supra* note 1, at 1531-51. *See, e.g., Receiver for Flagg*, POST-STAR (Glens Falls, N.Y.), May 2, 1917, at 7; *Fraudulent Stock Dealings*, ONEONTA (N.Y.) STAR, May 2, 1917, at 1; *Victims Share in Big Swindle of Jared Flagg*, STAR-GAZETTE (Elmira, N.Y.), May 4, 1917, at 10; *Flagg Creditors May Get Some Money Back*, ITHACA (N.Y.) J., May 7, 1917, at 6.

[34] *Receivers' Notice* (advertisement), N.Y. TIMES, May 19, 1917, at 16.

[35] Notice of Appeal and Assignment of Errors, in Transcript, *supra* note 1, at 1-9.

[36] *Id.*

[37] Citation, in Transcript, *supra* note 1, at 10.

[38] Affidavit [of Gilbert Roe] and Notice of Motion, Sept. 21, 1917, Cook v. Flagg, 251 F. 5 (2d Cir. 1918) (No. 297), on file at National Archives & Records Administration, Kansas City, Mo., Case File No. 6205, at 6.

[39] *Id.*

[40] *Id.* at 10.

[41] *Id.* at 14-15.

[42] Memorandum on Motion of Respondent to Dismiss Appeal, Oct. 2, 1917, Cook v. Flagg, 251 F. 5 (2d Cir. 1918) (No. 297), on file at National Archives & Records Administration, Kansas City, Mo., Case File No. 6205, at 1.

[43] Affidavits in Opposition, Oct. 2, 1917, Cook v. Flagg, 251 F. 5 (2d Cir. 1918) (No. 297), on file at National Archives & Records Administration, Kansas City, Mo., Case File No. 6205, at 3-5.

[44] Order, Oct. 15, 1917, Cook v. Flagg, 251 F. 5 (2d Cir. 1918) (No. 297), on file at National Archives & Records Administration, Kansas City, Mo., Case File No. 6205.

[45] Brief on Behalf of Defendant-Appellant, Jared Flagg, Dec. 10, 1917, Cook v. Flagg, 251 F. 5 (2d Cir. 1918) (No. 297), on file at National Archives & Records Administration, Kansas City, Mo., Case File No. 6205.

[46] Brief for Appellee, Dec. 10, 1917, Cook v. Flagg, 251 F. 5 (2d Cir. 1918) (No. 297), on file at National Archives & Records Administration, Kansas City, Mo., Case File No. 6205, at 12-13.

[47] *Id.* at 19-31.

[48] *Id.* at 31-44.

[49] *Id.* at 50-63.

[50] *Id.* at 67.

[51] GERALD GUNTHER, LEARNED HAND: THE MAN AND THE JUDGE 647 (1994).

[52] Cook v. Flagg, 251 F. 5 (1918). The opinion was originally filed on Jan. 16, 1918; a revised opinion, with minor edits, was filed on Feb. 21, but the original date has been retained in the published version. Copies of both are available at the National Archives & Records Administration, Kansas City, Mo., Case File No. 6205.

[53] *Id.* at 12 (citing Fiske v. Doucette, 92 N.E. 455 (Mass. 1910), Green v. Corey, 97 N.E. 70 (Mass. 1912) & Katz v. Nast, 187 F. 529 (7th Cir. 1910)).

[54] Motion for Rehearing on Behalf of Jared Flagg, Defendant-Appellant, Jan. 26, 1918, Cook v. Flagg, 251 F. 5 (2d Cir. 1918) (No. 297), on file at National Archives & Records Administration, Kansas City, Mo., Case File No. 6205, at 2-3.

[55] Motion for Rehearing on Behalf of Jared Flagg, Defendant-Appellant, Feb. 18, 1918, Cook v. Flagg, 251 F. 5 (2d Cir. 1918) (No. 297), on file at National Archives & Records Administration, Kansas City, Mo., Case File No. 6205, at 2-3.

[56] Order for Mandate, Feb. 26, 1918, Cook v. Flagg, 251 F. 5 (2d Cir. 1918) (No. 297), on file at National Archives & Records Administration, Kansas City, Mo., Case File No. 6205.

[57] Flagg v. Cook, 247 U.S. 508 (1918) (denying certiorari). *See also Flagg Decisions Sustained*, N.Y. Tribune, May 7, 1918, at 10.

[58] *See* Kaufman v. Jared Flagg Corp., 237 N.Y.S. 26 (App. Div. 1929).

[59] *Commercial Space Leased*, N.Y. Herald, April 7, 1918, at 82.

[60] E. Ellsworth Cook, Find A Grave, at https://www.findagrave.com/memorial/83323521/e.-ellsworth-cook. *See also Hotel Man of Shelbyville Dead*, JACKSONVILLE (ILL.) DAILY J., March 7, 1924, at 1; *Cook Funeral in Shelbyville*, DECATUR (ILL.) HERALD, March 10, 1924, at 2; *Cook Will Is Filed in Shelby County Court*, J. GAZETTE (Mattoon, Ill.), March 27, 1924, at 7.

Notes to Chapter 8

[1] JARED FLAGG, THE CRIMES OF JARED FLAGG 3 (1920). *See infra* text accompanying notes 9-11 in this chapter for a discussion of the two versions of CRIMES; the introduction, titled "To The Reader," noted here appears only in what is presumed here to be the later of the two, called Crimes II hereinafter.

[2] *Id.* In CRIMES I, however, Flagg reported that "The first and second editions of [FLAGG'S FLATS] were printed in 1909, the third edition in 1910." CRIMES I at 39.

[3] JARED FLAGG, FLAGG'S FLATS vii (1909) [hereinafter FLATS I].

[4] *Id.*

[5] JARED FLAGG, FLAGG'S FLATS ix (undated)[hereinafter FLATS II].

[6] *Id.* at iv.

[7] CRIMES II, *supra* note 1, at 320.

[8] *Id.*

[9] Library of Congress, Copyright Office, Catalog of Copyright Entries, Part 1, Books, Group 1, at 163 (April 1920); https://books.google.com/books?id=8ww DAAAAYAAJ&ppis=_c&lpg=PA163&dq=the%20crimes%20of%20jared%20f lagg&pg=PA163#v=onepage&q=the%20crimes%20of%20jared%20flagg&f=fa lse.

[10] CRIMES I, *supra* note 2. This version is available at http://www.archive.org/ details/crimesofjared00flag and the UCLA Library.

[11] CRIMES II, *supra* note 1.

[12] CRIMES I, *supra* note 2, at 75-76.

[13] *Id.* at 108-113.

[14] *Id.* at 205-211.

[15] *Id.* at 288-89.

[16] CRIMES II, *supra* note 1, at 159.

[17] CRIMES I, *supra* note 2, at 295.

[18] *Id.* at 299.

[19] *Id.* at 321.

[20] *Id.* at 323-33.

[21] *Id.* at 341.

[22] *Id.* at 342-44.

[23] *Id.* at 350. CRIMES II ends with: "And such are the 'crimes' of JARED FLAGG." CRIMES II, *supra* note 1, at 191.

[24] Testimony of Jared Flagg Before the Attorney General of the State of New York, Plaintiff's Exhibit 3, in Record on Appeal, at 536-37, Kaufman v. Jared Flagg Corp., 237 N.Y.S. 26 (App. Div. 1929), available at https://books.google. com/books?id=1GATPHFR31wC&pg=PP1&lpg=PP1&dq=AEZU-S38-UL2C& source=bl&ots=ENlCylXlyW&sig=ACfU3U2fxQlakDH_Pxy66Mrx_gngmHwa dw&hl =en&sa=X&ved=2ahUKEwif_Z-y9vLoAhV8l3IE HeGvDg8Q6AEwA

HoECAQQKA#v=onepage&q=AEZU-S38-UL2C&f=false [hereinafter Record on Appeal].

[25] *See* ch. 4, *supra,* text accompanying note 9.

[26] Testimony of Jared Flagg, *supra* note 24, at 537.

[27] Email from Peter Flagg Maxson, June 2020, on file with author.

[28] *New Owner for West Side House*, N.Y. TRIBUNE, Aug. 12, 1920, at 17; *Dwelling Sales Reported,* N.Y. HERALD, Aug. 12, 1920, at 17. Several of the buildings described here are still standing. The Second Church of Christ Scientist is now called the First Church of Christ Scientist, having merged with that congregation in 2003. The Hotel des Artistes is a 17-story cooperative apartment building with 119 units. And 14 West 68th Street currently houses offices of Accent Reduction— Speakwell, Speech and Language Pathologists, and, until 2001, the Partnership for Responsible Drug Information.

[29] Notice of Removal (undated), Plaintiff's Exhibit 3, in Record on Appeal, at 561.

[30] *See Plan West Side Dwellings*, N.Y. HERALD, Aug. 17, 1921, at 17.

[31] Testimony of Jared Flagg, *supra* note 24, at 538-39.

[32] Newspapers in the fall of 1921 and spring of 1922 reported various judgments outstanding against Jared Flagg. *See, e.g., Judgments, N.Y. Cnty.,* N.Y. TIMES, Nov. 11, 1921, at 18; *Judgments Filed, N. Y. Cnty.,* N.Y. TRIBUNE, April 8, 1922, at 18.

[33] Plaintiff's Exhibit 1, in Record, *supra* note 24, at 547.

[34] 6% Guaranteed Profit-Participation Gold Bond Certificate, Nov. 1, 1921, Exhibit B, Annexed to Complaint, in Record, *supra* note 24, at 28 *et seq.* [hereinafter Certificate].

[35] Plaintiff's Exhibit 1, in Record, *supra* note 24, at 547-561.

[36] Certificate, *supra* note 32.

[37] Opinion by Justice Mahoney, in Record, *supra* note 24, at 709.

[38] Kaufman v. Flagg Corp., 237 N.Y.S. 26, (1929).

[39] The Bureau was created to carry out the mandate of the state legislature to investigate fraud in the sale and circulation of bonds, stock certificates and other securities. Laws of 1921, ch. 649; *see In re* Ottinger, 148 N.E. 627 (N.Y. 1926).

[40] N.Y. Gen. Bus. L., art. 23-a.

[41] Testimony of Jared Flagg, *supra* note 24, at 536.

[42] Kaufman v. Flagg Corp., 237 N.Y.S. 26, 29 (1929).

[43] *Id.* at 280.

[44] Opinion by Justice Mahoney, in Record, *supra* note 24, at 708.

[45] *Id.* at 722.

[46] Kaufman v. Flagg Corp., 237 N.Y.S. 26, 28 (1929).

[47] *Id.* at 31.

[48] *Left $65,000*, ITHACA (N.Y.) J., Sept. 4, 1929, at 6.

[49] Email from Peter Flagg Maxson, *supra* note 27.

[50] *File Will of Broker Who Died on Grill*, BROOKLYN DAILY EAGLE, Sept. 12, 1926, at 22.

[51] Testimony of Ernest Flagg, in Record, *supra* note 24, at 257.

[52] Email from Peter Flagg Maxson, *supra* note 27.

[53] *See, e.g., Artist Flagg is Dead*, BALTIMORE SUN, Sept. 26, 1899, at 6; *Jared B. Flagg, Sr.,* ST. LOUIS GLOBE-DEMOCRAT, Sept. 26, 1899, at 2; *Death of Artist Jared B. Flagg Sr.,* CHICAGO TRIBUNE, Sept. 26, 1899, at 5; *Jared B. Flagg,* TIMES-PICAYUNE (New Orleans), Sept. 26, 1899, at 2; *New Yorker Nachrichten (New York News),* DER DEUTSCHE CORRESPONDENT (Baltimore), Sept. 26, 1899, at 3.

[54] Evarts served as Assistant U.S. Attorney in New York City, U.S. Attorney General, Secretary of State, and U.S. Senator. Miller Center, University of Virginia, https://millercenter.org/president/ hayes/evarts-1877-secretary-of-state.

[55] *Jared B. Flagg*, HARTFORD COURANT, Sept. 26, 1899, at 7.

[56] *Montague Flagg's Career Noted One*, HARTFORD COURANT, Dec. 26, 1915, at 7.

[57] *Charles N. Flagg, Noted Artist, Dead*, N.Y. TIMES, Nov. 11, 1916, at 9; *Artist Flagg Found Dead*, BROOKLYN DAILY EAGLE, Nov. 10, 1916, at 2.

[58] *He Wants $50,000 Damages*, N.Y. EVENING WORLD, June 6, 1889, at 4. Interestingly, the newspaper article refers to Charles Noël as "Young Flagg."

[59] There had been charges that Flagg's award of the architectural contract for the Corcoran was influenced by favoritism because of his family's prominence in the art world. MARDGES BACON, ERNEST FLAGG, BEAUX-ARTS ARCHITECT AND URBAN REFORMER 68 (1986).

[60] *Id.* at 72. *See also* ERNEST FLAGG & HARRY DESMOND, THE WORKS OF ERNEST FLAGG (2010); ERNEST FLAGG, FLAGG'S SMALL HOUSES, THEIR ECONOMIC DESIGN AND CONSTRUCTION (1922).

[61] *See, e.g., What is Doing in Society*, N.Y. TIMES, Nov. 9, 1900, at 7; *Society At Home and Abroad*, N.Y. TIMES, June 23, 1901, at 42; *The Morristown Horse Show Prizes*, N.Y. TRIBUNE, Sept. 13, 1901, at 5.

[62] *Washington Allston Flagg*, N.Y. TRIBUNE, Jan. 29, 1903, at 9.

[63] *Chas. Scribner, Publisher, Dies in 76th Year*, BROOKLYN DAILY EAGLE, April 20, 1930, at 1.

[64] *Mrs. Louise Scribner*, COURIER-NEWS (Bridgewater, N.J.)

[65] CECELIA TICHI, WHAT WOULD MRS. ASTOR DO? 288 (2018).

[66] Rosalie Allston Flagg Jaffray, Find A Grave, https://www.findagrave.com/memorial/182504629/ rosalie-allston-jaffray.

[67] Email from Peter Flagg Maxson, Architectural Historian, Austin, Tex., to the author (Sept. 22, 2018) (on file with author).

Index

A

A.C. Chamberlain & Son 12
Aborn Opera Co. 39-40
Actors' National Protective Union of America 44
Advice to Those Who Denounce the Stage 46
Allen, James 77, 80
Allston, Washington 3
American Steam Pump Co. 68
Andrews, Avery D. 28
Andrews, May 21
Archives of American Art, Smithsonian Institution 125
Arneff, Adam C. 82
Arthur, Helen 48
Ashland, W. 39-40
Astor, Caroline Schermerhorn 2, 127
Avery Architectural and Fine Arts Library, Columbia University 126

B

Bacon, Mardges 125
Baldwin, William D. 118
Barry, Minifred 123
Batcheldor, Mrs. (aka Olive Wilson, Olive Howard) 27
Baumann, Edna W. 118
Baumann, Jacob 15
Beatty, Robert C. 70, 77, 82. 84
Bentley, Bertha L. 62-63, 73
Bissell, Champion 12-14
Bogart, John N. 47-48
Bond, Josephine (Flagg) 4-5
Black Friday 5
Blair Brothers 62
Bookstaver, Judge Henry W. 18

Boyd v. United States 97-98
Bucket Shops 56
Breakers, The 3
Brooke, Charles W. 32-34
Brooklyn Daily Eagle 9, 11
Brooklyn, New York 3
Brooklyn Heights 3
Brown, David R. 12
Brown, Frederick 1
Brown, Joshua 64, 73, 77
Brown, Owen N. 95-96
Browne's Chop House 64
Bureau for the Prevention and Punishment of Fraud 1, 121

C

Café des Beaux Arts 63, 68
Campbell, S. 79
Canyon of Heroes 1
Carroll, Edward R. 50
Century Building 116
Chapman, Captain George S. 34
Charles Francis Press 77, 114-115
Childs, A. B. 84
City Hall Post Office 61
Cleveland Administration 60
Coleman, John M. 82-84, 86-89, 93-94, 96, 104, 112
Collins, Minturn Post 116
Columbia College 4
Connecticut Herald 3
Connecticut League of Art Students 124
Consolidated Exchange 62, 69, 77-78
Cook, Ellsworth E. 95, 101-113, 117
Co-operative Mutual Theatrical Agents Protective Association 38, 42, 44

Cooper, William J. 13
Corcoran Gallery of Art 125
Cornell, Magistrate Robert C. 28
Coxe, Judge Alfred C. 98-99
Court of Common Pleas 18
Court of General Sessions 22, 50
Court of Oyer and Terminer 28
Court of Special Sessions 22
Crimes of Jared Flagg, The 113-114,
  116-118, 127
Crook, Robert R. 55-56
Cullison, Webster 47
*Cyclones or The Power of
  Persuasion* 18-19

D

Daily Journal, The (Meriden,
  Connecticut)
Democrat and Chronicle, The
  (Rochester, New York) 56
Department of Licenses 42
DeWolf, Edward C. 74-75, 77
Dick & Fitzgerald 53
Dickson, Warren W. 62, 97
Donohue, Captain John J. 21-28
Dowling, Justice V. J. 48

E

École des Beaux-Arts 9
Ederle, Gertrude 1
Eighteenth Street Methodist
  Episcopal Church 23
Ellis, Wade H. 81, 84
Evarts, William M. 124
Evergreen Cemetary 123
*Evolution of an Equestrian Statue,
  The* 125

F

Farmers National Bank 94
Farrar, Thomas L. 55-56
Fellows, John R. 26, 28, 116
Fensler, J. P. 87
Flagg, Alice (Vanderbilt) 3
Flagg, Anna D. Robins 126

Flagg, Charles Noël 2-4, 12, 123-125
Flagg, Ebenezer 3
Flagg, Elise Cordier 124
Flagg, Eliza Longworth 127
Flagg, Ellen F. Earle 125
Flagg, Ernest 2-3, 6-7, 9, 49, 68-71,
  91, 104, 118, 123, 125-126
Flagg, George 3
Flagg, Gershom 3
Flagg, Henry Collins 3
Flagg, Henry Collins (Jr.) 3
Flagg, Jared Bradley 2-3, 6-7, 12, 18,
  123
Flagg, Jared (Jr.)
  *Advice to Those Who Denounce
  the Stage* 46
  Appeal of Conviction 93-100
  Birth 3
  Bissell, Conspiracy with 13-14
  Co-operative Apartments 9
  Cook v. Flagg 101-112, 117
  Crimes of Jared Flagg, The 113-
  114, 116-118
  Death 2, 122-123
  52% Flagg 51-71, 94-95
  Federal Trial 73-92
  Fire Extinguisher Business 10-11
  Fish Businesses 6-7, 12, 116
  Flagg Raid, The 76, 115-117
  Flagg's Flats 49, 67, 113-117
  Flagg's Philosophies 85
  Flats for Immoral Purposes 21-35
  Furniture Business 14-20
  How to Solve the Social Problem
  30
  *How to Take Money Out of Wall
  Street* 12, 51, 53, 55, 84, 105
  "Hypocrisy" 9
  Jared Flagg Company, The 56, 85,
  118
  Jared Flagg Corporation, The
  118-123
  Judgments Against 12
  Lectures 9
  Questioned 1-2

Real Estate Development 12
Theatrical Agency 37-51
Tombs, The 2, 13, 34, 64, 66
Wall Street 4-7, 13
Flagg, John 3
Flagg, Josephine Bond 4-5
Flagg, Louisa Hart 3-4, 127
Flagg, Louise (Scribner) 2, 4, 126-127
Flagg, Martha 3
Flagg, Montague 2-4, 12, 68, 124
Flagg, Rachel Moore 3
Flagg, Rosalie Allston (Jaffray) 2, 4
Flagg, Sarah Robbins Montague 3
Flagg, Washington Allston 2-3, 7, 126
Flagg, William J. 127
Flagg Raid, The 76, 115-117
Flagg's Flats 49, 67, 113-117
Flagg's Philosophies 85
Flegg, Thomas 3
Fifth Amendment 83, 93, 96-98
Fifth Avenue Plaza Apartments 8
Fire Extinguisher Patent 10-11
Fisk, Jim 5
Forgotten Books 114
Fourth Amendment 96-98
Foster, Charles 124
France, Rev. J. C. 79
Francis, Charles 114
Frank E. Campbell Funeral Chapel 123

G

Galbraith, Edward A. 10-11
Gilchrist, Commissioner Alexander
    J. 64, 70, 73, 97
Gilded Age 2
Goodhart, Laurence G. 47-48
Google Books 114
Gotham 20
Gould, Jay 5
Grace Church 3
Grand Central Palace 45
Grant, Ulysses S. 5

Great Northern Railway 55

H

Hammerstein, Oscar 37, 39-41
Hand, Judge Augustus N. 103-107,
    109
Hand, Judge Learned 80, 111
Hankey, Rufus P. 77
Hanna, William 50
Harris, Elmer E. 74
Hart, Louisa (Flagg) 3-4, 127
Hartford, Connecticut 3, 123-124
Hartford Courant, The 123-124
Hastings, Pauline 22
Hatfield, Augustus 9
Hayward Hand Grenade Co. 11
Herald, The (New York) 17
Henkel, Marshal William 63, 69-70,
    96
Henry Thousen & Co. 19
Higgins, Alvin M. 64, 67, 73, 77
Hitchcock, Frank H. 69
Holland House 105
Hopkins Grammar School 4
Hotel des Artistes 118
Hough, Judge Charles M. 73, 81,
    103, 105
Howard, Olive (aka Olive Wilson,
    Mrs. Batcheldor) 27
How to Solve the Social Problem 32
*How to Take Money Out of Wall
    Street* 12, 51, 53, 55, 84, 105
Hubert, Philip G. 7
"Hypocrisy" 9

I

Iden, F. H. 79
Ingersoll, Robert 9
Ingraham, Justice Daniel P. 28

J

J. & S. Baumann Furniture 15, 17
Jared Flagg Company, The 56, 85,
    118

Jared Flagg Corporation, The 118-123
Jarvis, Robert M. 62
Jackson, Henry A. 55-56, 62, 64, 73, 77, 118-121
Jaffray, Rosalie Allston Flagg 2, 127
Jaffray, William Dexter 127
Jefferson Street Market Courthouse & Prison 21
Jerome, William Travers 44-45, 47
Johnes & Travis 18

K

Kauffman, J. W. 121-122
Keating, Frederick L. C. 42-46
Keating, Neil McLeod 125
Kehoe, Michael 82
Kenny's Restaurant 24
Keyes, Lillian Gibbs 62
Kilbreth, James T. 13
Kincaid, Elmer L. 62-63, 69, 96-97
Koch, Theodore W. 114

L

Lackawanna Railroad 55
Lacombe, Emile Henry 69-70, 76, 83, 95
La Follette, Sen. Robert 102
Lammot, Eugene 13
Lawrence, Joseph M. 45
Leavitt & Grant 62
Leggett, Francis H. 26
Lehigh Valley Cement Co. 12
Lexow Committee 23, 26
Lexow, Sen. Clarence 23
Lewis, (Assistant District Attorney) 30, 33
License Law 44
Lindsay, John D. 27
Littleton, Martin W. 95-97
Louis Jacquesson de la Chevreuse 124
Ludwig Baumann Furniture 15

M

M. Witmark & Sons 39-40
MacFarlane, Wallace 104
Mackie, Willis & Co 13-14
Madison Square 21
Mahoney, Justice Jeremiah T. 122
Manhattan Life Insurance Building 1, 121
Manufacturers Trust Co. 1
Marshall, H. Snowden 83-84, 96-99, 192
Martens, Captain _____ 25
Martin Act 121
Mayer, Judge Julius M. 111
Maxson, Marion Flagg 127
Maxson, Peter Flagg 127
McClure, S. S. 103
McConville, Bernard 22, 28, 30, 33
McDonald & Co. 62
McIntyre, John F. 74
Metropolitan Job Printing Co. 12
Mildeberger, H.D. 48, 85-87, 104, 106, 117
Miller Syndicate 65-66
Mitchell, Bessie 27
Mitchell, Minnie 27
Mitchell Public Library 114
Moller, J. W. 118
Montague, Sarah Robbins (Flagg) 3
Morford, Thomas E. 68-69
Morgan, Daniel N. 60, 64, 67, 69, 73, 77, 88
Morgan, J.P. 56
Murphy, Delia 21
Murray, Hazel 74

N

National Academy of Design Exhibition of 1908
Neely, F. Tennyson 62, 64, 73, 77
Newberger, Justice Joseph E. 30-34
New Haven, Connecticut 3-4, 123
New Haven Daily Morning Journal & Courier 11
New Haven Pipe Co. 12
Newport, Rhode Island 3

New York Stock Exchange 62, 65,
  78

O

O'Malley, Justice James 122
Ottinger, Albert 1, 121

P

Palmer, (Tams Agency) 40
Panama Canal 44
Panic of 1869 5
Panic of 1907 57
Parkhurst, Dr. Charles H. 22, 26, 30,
  43, 47, 60
Park Row Building 77, 116
Paris Salon of 1878 124
Paterno, The 58
Pavilion Summer Theater 9
Pettybone [sic], Al 53
Plaza Hotel 3, 8
Ponzi, Charles 59
Post & Flagg 7, 126
Post, Jr., George B. 126
Potter, William A. 8
Pratt, Mary 114
Price, Captain James K. 25-27
Protective Committee 76

R

R. J. Horner & Co. 17-18
Rand, _____ 74, 117
Reading Railroad 54-55
Real Estate Record & Guide 8
Reed, William B. 68
Robert L. Cutting & Co. 7
Robins Conveying Belt Company
  126
Roe, Gilbert E. 101-106, 108-110,
  112-113, 117, 122
Rogers, Judge Henry Wade 111
Roosevelt, Theodore 26, 30, 47, 60
Rudkin, Judge Frank H. 82-84, 86-
  90, 93-94, 96
Russe, Belle 68, 75, 77

Russe, Madeline 68-69, 73-75, 91,
  93, 118

S

St. Louis Exposition of 1904 124
St. Paul, Minnesota 4
St. Paul Railroad 55
Salter, Ilma 39
Samuels, Philip C. 106-109
Schiller, Edward L. 55-56, 64, 68,
  73, 77
Schock, Rev. James T. 55-56, 64, 73,
  77, 80
Scribner, Charles (II) 2, 124, 127
Scribner, Louise Flagg 2, 126-127
Second Church of Christ Scientist
  118
Sewall, Elbridge C. 68, 73, 77, 88
She is the Sunshine of Paradise Alley
  35, 44
Shill, Henry W. 26, 28
Smith, Abel F. 64
Smith, Charlotte Odlum 48
Smith, George D. 38, 46
Star, The (New York) 16
Storey Cotton Co. 65
Southern District of New York 90,
  101
Sun, The (New York) 42-44, 51, 53,
  105
Surrogate's Court 123

T

Tammany Hall 60
Tams Agency 40
Terwilliger & Peck 12
Tenderloin, The 21
Theodore R. Proctor Prize 125
Thompson, Claude A. 73-74, 77, 81-
  86, 88-90, 93, 115-1176
Ticker and Investment Digest, The 54
Tilden Building 58
Times, The (New York) 51, 73, 107
Todd, L. L. 9
Tombs, The 2, 13, 34, 64, 66

Tribune, The (New York) 65
Trinity College 4
Trumbull, Grover C. 87

U

Union Pacific Railroad 54-55
United States Court of Appeals for
    the Second Circuit 98-100, 105,
    107-108, 111
United States Naval Academy 125
United States Supreme Court 83-85,
    112
United States v. Weeks 83, 98-99
University of Michigan Library 114

V

Vanderbilt, Alice Flagg 3
Vanderbilt, Commodore Cornelius 3-
    4, 9, 124
Vanderbilt, Cornelius (II) 3, 124
Veeder, Judge Van Vechten 99
Verplanck, J. D. 80
Victoria Theater 37, 39
Vigilance League 22-23

W

Waldorf-Astoria Hotel 56
Walter Russell, Penrhyn Stanlaws,
    and Associates 118
Ward, Judge Henry G. 99
Weeks, Bartow S. 31, 115-116
West Side Savings Bank 121
Wheeler, Evelyn 43
Wilson, Dr. John A. B. 23-24, 28-29
Wilson, Olive (aka Olive Howard,
    Mr. Batcheldor) 27
Winans, John 6
Wise, Henry A. 64, 68-70, 95-96
Winslow, William B. 104, 106
Winter, Keyes 1-2, 121-122
Witmark, Marcus 39
Woman's Municipal League 47-48
Woman's Rescue League 47-48
Wood, Julia E. 73
Work, Ellen Wood 5

Work, Frank 5, 53
World, The (New York) 12-15, 57-
    58, 66, 74, 90, 117
Wycoff, Richard D. 53

Y

Yale University 4

Z

Ziegler, Irving E. 64